PUBLIC ACCESS TO LIBRARY AUTOMATION

Papers presented at the 1980 Clinic on Library Applications
of Data Processing, April 20-23, 1980

Clinic on Library Applications
of Data Processing: 1980

Public Access to Library Automation

Edited by
J.L. DIVILBISS

Graduate School of Library and Information Science
University of Illinois at Urbana-Champaign

Library of Congress Cataloging in Publication Data

Clinic on Library Applications of Data Processing
(17th : 1980 : University of Illinois at Urbana-
Champaign)
Public access to library automation

Includes index.
1. Libraries--Automation--Congresses. 2. Library
science--Data processing--Congresses. 3. Libraries
and readers--Congresses. I. Divilbiss, J. L.
II. University of Illinois at Urbana-Champaign.
Graduate School of Library and Information Science.
III. Title.
Z678.9.A1C5   1981   025.3'028'54   81-11685
ISBN 0-87845-065-3   AACR2

CONTENTS

Introduction

Of the various trends in library automation today, public access is clearly one of the most difficult, complex, and potentially rewarding areas of development. The motivation may be economic or it may be the desire to offer a new standard of service; in either case the designer of a public access system finds himself in largely uncharted waters. In planning the 1980 clinic, we attempted to bring together speakers who could address both the philosophical foundations and the nuts-and-bolts reality of public access. As an example of the former, Shaw points out how little we know about public use of automated systems. He then makes the persuasive argument that our best chance for understanding and improving man-machine communication is through heuristics. Hewett and Meadow continue this theme with a detailed discussion of an experiment to determine how effective an overlaid analysis and assistance program could be to untrained users of an information retrieval system. Their encouraging results have implications that extend to many other areas of public access. In her paper, Beckman describes the practical considerations that arise in providing public access in a university library. In summary, the common theme of these papers is that providing well-designed public access systems will be an uncommonly challenging task, but that early results give us cause for great optimism.

J.L. DIVILBISS
Editor

WARD SHAW

Executive Director

Colorado Alliance of Research Libraries

Design Principles for Public Access

Basically, the problem of designing an information system for public access is the same as the problem of designing any kind of system, and perhaps can be stated as a question: How do we construct or plan that interaction of hardware, software, people, and data that will be most likely to lead to a predetermined good or goal? Ideally, we should have a fairly good idea of what the goal is, an understanding of the mechanism of the change required to meet the goal, and a comprehension of the characteristics of the interactions of hardware, software, people, and data, so that we may apply those characteristics to the design and control of the events necessary to cause the change desired. Traditionally stated, this means: define the output, define the input, and then invent a process that will transform the input into the output.

The trouble is that when it comes to the design of information systems, and particularly public access information systems, it is extraordinarily difficult to reach clear definitions of *output* or *input*; and, moreover, nearly impossible to define a process that will transform one into the other. That is why it is fundamentally easier to design a system to send a man to the moon by 1970 than to design an information system . You know where the moon is, and can learn a great deal about its characteristics. You know what a man is, and much about what his biology enables him to do; you know when 1970 is; and there exists a corpus of knowledge of mechanics that allows construction of a process that will get the man to the moon— that is, the problem is well defined and a solution is at least comprehensible. What remains is essentially a mechanistic exercise. However, in designing information systems, it is not enough to define input as those keys which a user strikes on a keyboard, and output as those records or messages which appear on a screen—surely we must pay attention to those things, but they do not treat the whole system. Information, like most "-tion" words, is a process—specifically, that process by which people become informed. Therefore, input becomes "an uninformed person" and output becomes "an informed person." But those are very fuzzy concepts, and that is particularly true of systems for public access. The basic difference between systems for public access and systems for "private" access is that, in the latter case, the designer can assume boundaries and hence some specification of the "uninformedness" of the user. He can also assume a certain degree of understanding by the user of what the system is supposed to do, and through that, can reduce his problem to that of defining a data retrieval or manipulation system. But in the case of systems for public access, such assumptions are perilous at best, because many different users of many different degrees of confusion will attempt to use the system for many different things; success will be measured not by such easily quantifiable things as relevance/recall ratios or numbers of documents delivered, but rather by user satisfaction.

To confuse the issue further, we don't know much about the process of informing, that is, how uninformed people become informed people. We do know that the process is closely related to, or perhaps equivalent to, learning, but we also know that educational theory is notoriously inadequate in describing exactly how to cause learning to occur. To return to something tangible, consider some of the questions that ought to be addressed in designing a computer-based public access information system—for example, a catalog:

1. How fast should system response be? Should the terminal display messages at reading speed so that users can read along as the terminal is responding, or should messages appear all at once for the user to read at pleasure? (If you think this simple characteristic is unimportant, try an interactive system at 300 baud and then try the same system at 9600 baud. You'll likely find that the system "feels" completely different, and that this "feel" affects your perception of it and its utility. But which is better, for what kinds of interactions?)

2. How much data, in what detail, should be presented, and at what stage of the interaction? If you present bibliographic records, how many elements are necessary? When does the format get in the way of useful information?

3. How much should users by involved in or control the interactive process? In a catalog, should the user who enters "Mark Twain" be informed that the correct name is Samuel Clemens and that the system will proceed with Clemens, or should the system substitute Twain for Clemens automatically, or should (for pedagogical purposes) the

system require the user to acknowledge (or even retype) the change to "Clemens"? What is the specific effect on the informing process of each of these options?

4. When should the system quit? That is, at what point can the user be considered to be "informed" and how is this measured? If left to user control, will he choose to quit before he "should" (for example, before the system directs him to periodical resources in addition to monographs)? Or is it better to make the system totally passive in this regard?

Clearly, the problem of identifying principles of system design for public access is a difficult one, and we certainly do not know enough about public access information systems to generate very many "rules" that can be applied a priori to guarantee a "good" system design. How, then, do we proceed?

We really know only three ways to approach design. The most frequently used, and usually the best, is the algorithmic method. This method is characterized by the systematic application of rules or formulas which will lead to the desired results. But, as we have seen, in the case of public access information systems, we don't understand enough about information-seeking behavior and the informing process to use this method successfully. In fact, we will probably generate this knowledge only through analysis of the use of many public access information systems over a considerable time; and, if the analogy to learning holds, we may never understand the process.

The second method is simulation. This method consists of creating a model of whatever it is you want to learn about (in this case, an information system). The model must have two characteristics: (1) it must represent the real world accurately with regard to significant variables, and (2) it must be capable of being efficiently and repeatedly exercised. The process is to run the model many times, each time changing one of the variable values, to learn which changes produce desirable results and which produce undesirable results. The problem is that it is very difficult to identify the relevant variables in information-seeking behavior, and much more difficult to derive accurate and representative relationships among those variables. We simply do not have a very good model available, nor does it appear likely that we will get one soon.

The third approach to design is the heuristic method, and I believe it to be the most promising approach to the design of systems for public access. Essentially, the heuristic methodology is as follows: in a case in which the designer does not understand enough about the mechanisms of a particular situation to invent appropriate algorithms—e.g., the case of public access systems—he generates a number of statements of value, or targets, which he believes will lead to desirable results. These statements of value are called heuristics, and perhaps the most common examples of systems developed using this approach are many of the chess-playing programs. It is clearly impractical to design algorithmic chess-playing programs. There are too many possible moves for even the fastest computer to evaluate. So, heuristics are developed—for example, "it is desirable to take your opponent's pawns," or "it is desirable to trade pieces of lower mobility for pieces of higher mobility," or "it is desirable to move powerful pieces quickly to the front." These moves will not guarantee that the program will win chess games, but most players believe that they are likely to lead to success. Thus, the designer develops his program to evaluate a few possible moves in any given situation, measuring their value by determining which of the heuristics they might satisfy. Value in the case of chess can, of course, be represented numerically, and the program can "score" possible moves to identify the "best" one.

A key element of the heuristic approach is feedback. Heuristics or value statements are developed and assigned a particular numeric value at the beginning of system use. The system, as it is exercised, monitors its success, and by tracking itself, modifies the numeric values or weights assigned to its various heuristics, seeking more frequent success. In this sense, then, the chess programs are self-modifying and "learn" from experience, becoming more and more likely to win. Of course, how good they get depends in considerable measure on how intelligently the original heuristics were selected, and it is therefore axiomatic that the software be designed for easy modification so that new heuristics can be added and useless ones removed.

Let's look again at the example of designing a public access catalog. We don't know exactly how to produce informed (or satisfied) users; that is to say, we do not understand the mechanisms by which uninformed users are transformed into informed users. Consequently, it is difficult to see how to apply the algorithmic method to the design of public access catalogs. We furthermore do not have a model of the information process that yields much confidence in its "goodness of fit," and so the simulation method does not appear very helpful. But we can identify heuristics— statements of value—about the behavior of an information system which might lead toward informed users, and if that is so, the heuristic method of design is probably the best bet. Remember that we are looking at the information system as a whole—not simply the hardware and software, but also the users and the data.

At the design level, there are many heuristics that might be identified. Following are a few examples, not intended to be exhaustive by any means, but rather illustrative. These statements may or may not be true, but do begin to describe a corpus of system characteristics which will lead directly to an initial system specification and a description of a process for system evolution or "self-tuning" as described above. First, there are a number of things we might say about the interaction of users with the rest of the system.

1. It is desirable (i.e., will lead to information) that the system allow the user maximum entry possibilities. That means that, for example, it is better to have indexes to ten data elements than to have indexes to five data elements. Thus, if you are deciding whether to provide access to the bibliographic records by ISBN, it is desirable to do so. Note that these kinds of decisions involve trade-offs, and the set of heuristics or value statements provides a framework for formalizing, controlling and eventually enhancing those trade-offs.

2. It is desirable that the user be able to ask the system for help at any point in the interaction, and that the help supplied be relevant. This means that a general-purpose "help" file is inadequate. Explanatory information presented to users should reflect where they are in the interaction, the path they have taken to get there, and the substantial data they are working with. This will probably require some code to generate appropriate responses on a semi-individual basis.

3. It is desirable that the user control the interaction, i.e., the user should feel like he is driving the machine rather than the other way around. The idea is that the machine should be responsive to the user.

4. It is desirable that the machine react to the user at the user's skill level. Novice users may need considerable instruction and step-by-step guidance during the interaction, but skilled users should not be confronted with repetition of instructions they already know.

5. It is desirable that the machine respond with data that appropriately answer a user's need. Messages should neither overwhelm nor "underwhelm" users. For example, if a freshman asks for a book on American education, it is not helpful for the machine to respond with bibliographic listings of all 600 of them. On the other hand, if someone wants a technical discussion of Rommel's Africa campaign, a response directing them to a general history of war is likely to be less than informative.

These are examples of statements that will allow basic design decisions to be made from the point of view of the users of the system. All involve trade-offs, all may or may not be true, and all may prove to be impossible, but they at least provide a framework for design decisions.

Similarly, there are any number of heuristics relating to the hardware/software area, and examples of these are presented below. Because one of the important considerations in heuristic design is the ability of the system to change, the first four examples relate to flexibility.

1. It is desirable to structure hardware and software in a modular fashion. The idea is that pieces of the system can be easily modified without dire

consequences to the rest of the system.

2. It is desirable that constant values be passed to software as variable values. A specific case of this is table-driven terminal control, and the benefit is that the constant values can be easily changed to meet different circumstances.

3. It is desirable that message content and message form be separated. For example, in designing screens it is far easier to deal with one software unit which formats information and another which collects the variable data to be presented than to deal with both at once.

4. It is desirable that data structures be as flexible as possible. As soon as you have designed an on-line catalog, someone will come along and insist that you turn it into a circulation system as well. If, for example, you are restricted by design to fixed-length records of fixed-length fields, this becomes difficult to accomplish.

5. It is desirable that terminals have considerable graphics capability. This will lead to increased capabilities. Some kinds of data are best presented in text or list form, but consider the difficulty of describing a map over the telephone. In that case, a picture does the job far better. This is probably also the case with exposing the syndetic structure of a catalog to its users.

6. It is desirable to minimize the time the machine spends accessing Disk files. The most common critical, limiting bottleneck in on-line biblio-graphic systems is the time the machine spends accessing index records and bibliographic records from disks, and the designer will do wonders for response time by attending to this at the design stage.

These, then, are examples of heuristics that, taken together and expanded, will probably lead to successful designs. None are true a priori, but we believe that they may lead to successful design.

The process, therefore, is to select a set of heuristics, and carefully state them. These will describe characteristics of the hardware, software, data, and interaction which the designer believes will lead to a successful system. The next step is to assign some relative value to each statement. The result will be a mechanism for making design decisions and trade-offs. Then, using these valued heuristics, the system can be designed. It can then be tested and, based on the results, the heuristics and the values assigned to them can be modified. In a continuous process, the system implementation will be changed to reflect these changed values. This recursive process, it is hoped, will at some point stabilize. At that point, the heuristics and associated values will become potential principles of design for public access. The heuristic method, then, is a codification of and control mecha-nism for the rough-and-ready approach that says "put something up and then tinker with it"—and I believe it offers the best hope of developing and learning about successful public access systems.

ALLEN AVNER
Senior Specialist in Automated Education
Director of Evaluation
Computer-based Education Research Laboratory
University of Illinois at Urbana-Champaign

H. GEORGE FRIEDMAN, JR.
Associate Professor of Computer Science
University of Illinois at Urbana-Champaign

Interacting with Computer Users: Design Considerations

The design of computer terminals which communicate with naïve users in a humane yet effective manner involves problems that are common to many applications. Interactive computers are being used as everyday tools in settings that range from airlines to zoos. The problems met by the growing use of computer terminals in libraries are seldom unique to that setting. In fact, the experience of the authors over the past two decades suggests the existence of a set of design problems that turn up whenever interactive computer terminals are used, whatever the setting. These hindrances emanate from inappropriate dependence on a few simplifying assumptions that make design easier at the cost of lowered effectiveness. This paper outlines six of these fallacious assumptions, describes the reasons for their beguiling attractiveness, and suggests alternative views that should lead to better design.

Human-Machine System Design

Human-machine interactions may be considered to consist of four major elements: task, procedure, human, and machine. The good system designer does not assume that any of these elements is a static, unchangeable factor that can be ignored. A thorough analysis may even reveal alternative approaches which eliminate the need for a special design.

Task

The task is the problem that is to be solved. A common error is the failure to understand that past views of the problems may have been limited by what was possible with tools and procedures then available.

New tools may make it possible to solve a larger problem. Where this is the case, the task should be defined to include factors not addressed by former approaches. An example common in computerization is that a computer brought in to simplify paperwork also turns out to be able to solve a part of the management process that the paperwork supported. Thus, a computer brought in to automate the production of book purchase orders would also be able to automate many of the standard administrative decisions made in following up on overdue deliveries. However, this added capability is likely to be included in the design of the system only if the designer is aware of the total task.

Procedure

Procedures are the methods used to complete a task. A common error is the confusion of procedures with tasks. A procedure (such as filling out a charge slip for a book by hand) comes to be seen as a required part of an operation, rather than as simply one of several means of performing the actual task (maintaining a record of changes in responsibility for a book). This particular confusion often results in technological misapplications that meet task needs by the simple, but usually inefficient, expedient of mimicking old procedures.

Another form of confusion of task and procedure results in the endowment of a procedure with almost magical powers. Thus, "computerization" may be cited as the reason for success of a new approach. That success is then used as the reason for blindly adopting computers in other situations without taking the trouble to determine what alternatives might be available. One result of such blind adoption of computers is the growing number of cases where an administrator "computerizes" an operation, shows great savings in time and money, and is promoted. He is then replaced by a new administrator who is miraculously able to eliminate the computer without losing the advantages of "computerization"! If the first administrator had taken the time to examine the actual task and the possible alternatives, he would have observed that all that was really needed was a restructuring of the task. The apparent gains derived from computerization in such cases really result from the task restructuring that accompanies the unnecessary addition of a computer. The computer can be dropped from such an implementation with minimal effect on working efficiency and substantial savings in cost. Needless to say, cost savings would have been even greater if the computer had never entered the scene.

Human

Humans appear in many roles in human-machine systems. They may help the machine carry out procedures, or they may be clients served by the

Figure 1. Beware of technological innovations that simply mimic old procedures.

Illustrations for this paper were drawn by Wayne Wilson, Computer-based Education Research Laboratory, University of Illinois at Urbana-Champaign.

system. The major error lies in ignoring the human element. A designer may assume that since he or she is human, any system design will automatically include all needed human factors. That is not so. Humans vary enormously in training, motivation and ability. Not only do they vary individually, but they vary with time. A system designed for naïve users may not be efficient for experienced users. Users who begin as naïve users will seldom remain that way with time. A system that is comfortable for brief human use can be an unbearable burden when used continuously for long hours. Good design demands a clear view of the nature of the humans who will interact with the system and the nature of that interaction.

Machine

The word *machine* is used here because we happen to be discussing computers. A more accurate word would be *tool*. The machine or tool is a technological aid to application of the procedure. A pencil or an instructional technique is just as valid a form of technology as a computer. It is a mistake to assume that some complex form of technology is needed for every task. As was noted above, careful restructuring of a work situation can result in substantial improvements in productivity without any need for a computer or other expensive technology.

Modularization

Once the major components of a human/machine process have been identified, good design practice dictates that the resulting system be further broken down into functional modules that cut across these major components. Each functional module performs a single distinct function in the solution of the overall task. A particular module is defined by the portion of the total task that it covers, the procedures needed to address that subtask, and the human and/or machine carrying out those procedures. Each module has well-defined inputs and outputs, and most modules interact only with other modules.

Modularization is not done simply in response to an innate drive of system designers to categorize things. Modularization allows concurrent development of the many parts of a complex system by different groups of designers operating in relative independence, thus greatly reducing the length of time between initial planning and putting a system into operation. Modularization also has advantages in the completed product.

Both hardware (the terminals, computers and other devices associated with the system) and software (the computer programs which guide the hardware and interpret interactions between hardware and humans) can be modularized. Modularized hardware is easier to maintain, since modules that serve only a single, well-defined function are easier to isolate should they malfunction. Modules are also amenable to quick, inexpensive repair by substitution. Properly designed modular hardware is also more easily altered or expanded to meet changing needs of a given installation. For example, needs for additional terminals or increased information storage capability can be met simply by adding the needed equipment and the control modules required to interface it with the original system. The same expansion in a nonmodularized system might require major redesigning of both hardware and software. Modularized software has similar advantages in identification and repair of problems and in modification of existing installations.

Unfortunately, the advantages of modularization can cause a designer to downgrade the importance of other design considerations. For example, modularization is easiest when the task structure is relatively simple and when there are few interactions between tasks or procedures of different types. In seeking such simplicity, a good system designer tries to eliminate extraneous elements from the task that the system is to perform. Under time pressure, however, such commendable parsimony can lead to over-simplification. Oversimplification results either from failures of commission (misinterpreting a user's description of the task) or failures of omission (failing to verify that an interpretation of the task actually leads to an acceptable final result). The fault in failures of omission is not always with the system designer alone. A user who is not familiar with the computer's slavishly literal interpretation of directives may fail to specify the crucial decisions that are often made by a human faced with ambiguous information. A human is able to make commonsense interpretations that may result in the job's completion despite less than ideal information. A computer programmed with an oversimplified procedure for handling the same ambiguous data may merrily grind out stacks of absolute rubbish. Eventually such failures will come to light, of course, but it is far more efficient to identify them at the time the system design is being specified. In the early design stages, no amount of experience in computer system design can replace the knowledgeable guidance of a person who has actually carried out the original task under "real-life" conditions.

With this general background, let us examine six of the most common fallacies that intrude on the design of interactive computer terminal systems. We hope that once you are aware of these pitfalls to good design, you will be better able to guide design or selection of an interactive terminal system that will meet the special needs of your application.

The Fallacy of Subsystem Independence

The person following this erroneous design principle assumes that any component of a system can be designed effectively without any knowledge of the rest of the system. It is both convenient and useful to handle design of a system by breaking the major system into component modules. This does not mean, however, that the final system is intended to function as a set of independent modules.

Problems of the "Fallacy of Subsystem Independence" show themselves most frequently in hardware interactions. At the lowest level, the user might encounter massive delays in accessing or storing information at a terminal that is mismatched to a communications channel or storage device. The fact that two such components can be made to communicate with each other by means of intermediate software or hardware does not necessarily mean that the interaction will be efficient.

At a more complex (and, unfortunately, more often observed) level, a system might perform a variety of functions quite well when the system is supporting only one user. However, a system which has not been designed as an integrated whole may show severely degraded performance when asked to support different operations simultaneously by several users at different interactive terminals. It may even degrade severely simply as a result of user loads above some moderate level.

The Fallacy of System Function

The motto of the believer in this fallacy is "If it works, the design is okay." No designer intentionally designs a system that is difficult to use, performs inefficiently, or assumes an inordinate amount of skill on the part of the user. Nevertheless, under pressure to produce a functioning system while facing the ever present time deadlines and funding limitations that mark reality, designers are too frequently willing to accept almost anything that actually gets the intended task done. They may have started out with far grander intentions and an abiding desire to produce a system that would be both a joy to use and a paragon of efficiency. But in the cold, hard dawn of reality (and corporate solvency), they may have been willing to compromise with something that met the minimum specifications of the contract.

Given the tendency of humans to compromise when under pressure, it is wise to make sure that minimal contractual specifications will actually provide acceptable levels of performance in the finished system. To insure that minimal specifications are adequate, one must go beyond simple statements of input information and output products. One must identify important conditional factors such as speed and ease of operation, and specify the operating condition under which these performance levels are expected.

A system must be expected to perform differently under different usage loads. In recognition of this fact of life, the levels of performance required under a "normal" load and under the most severe load anticipated should both be specified. We must always remember that even if a system "works" (i.e., produces the desired results under ideal conditions), it will not necessarily be acceptable to users (i.e., produce the desired results in a real life setting).

The Fallacy of Human Perspicacity

This fallacy is committed by most persons involved with the design of interactive systems. The assumption that all humans will think exactly the way *you* think (and that they will automatically understand your intent at each step of an interaction) is woefully common. The more involved a designer becomes with the mechanics of getting a system to "work," the more he or she grows accustomed to the idiosyncratic manner in which it happens to operate at that moment. After a while, the designer forgets that everyone will not come to the system with a full understanding of the intent behind each human-machine interaction.

Figure 2. A foot-thick instruction manual is no substitute for good human-machine design.

The day of reckoning arrives with the first use by people who were not involved with the original design. If the designers are wise, such people will be brought in well before the design of human-machine interactions has been frozen. Careful study of the problems encountered by naïve users will greatly aid in reducing potential errors and in increasing the ease of interaction. If the designers are *not* wise, they will delay exposure of the system to realistic field testing until final delivery of the system. Systems designed under this "blind" approach are most notable for their literary contributions—a frantic, last-minute effort to compensate for poor human engineering by provision of a flood of instruction manuals. In general, the less often a user interacts with a computer terminal, the less voluminous the printed instruction manuals should be. A well-designed interactive computer system provides complete interactive prompting for the new or infrequent user. Ideally, one should be able to start a new user by simply saying, "Follow the directions on that screen." Assuming reasonably literate users, anything less than this should be taken as a possible sign of limitations either in hardware capabilities or, more likely, in software design.

The Fallacy of Human Memory

A fallacy which is particularly prevalent in the design of information and instruction displays for interactive terminal systems is the assumption that humans can remember every detail of information encountered several minutes or even seconds before. This fallacy is actually a special case of the "Fallacy of Human Perspicacity" and is perpetrated for the same reason. After many days of working with the structure of a system, one forgets that someone seeing the system for the first time will, for example, actually be using instructions as sources of new information and not simply as mile markers on a familiar path.

In the brief exchanges characteristic of use of interactive computer terminals, humans depend mostly on short-term memory. This is the same type of memory that we use for tasks such as remembering a telephone number from the time we look it up in a directory to the time we dial it on the telephone. Short-term memory normally has a very limited capacity (about three to four simple items or groups of items) and is easily overwritten by new information.[1] It is not reasonable to expect people to take the time to memorize directions on a display which they have little intention of using frequently. Nor, given the limitations of short-term memory, is it reasonable to expect a human to remember an item of information from one display and combine it with information from another display. While this is a task that *can* be done, it is a task that forces a human to do something a computer can do far better.

Well-designed interactions provide directions appropriate to the needs of the user at the moment they are needed. Well-designed interactions also keep track of information acquired by the user (e.g., in a search procedure) and permit easy recovery of that information. For example, after completing a complex search operation, the user should be able to make a minor change in specifications and start a new search without having to retype the full set of specifications.

The Fallacy of Human Patience

Time is probably the most frequently overlooked incidental factor in system performance. Designs that ignore the effect of delays in system response on user acceptance or performance are implicitly assuming that such effects do not exist. Rest assured, they do. Short delays—for example, when a user types a letter and nothing appears immediately on the display—can convince the user that the system has not seen an input. Delays as short as a quarter-second can lead users to make repeated inputs. The repeated input leads in turn to errors (a double letter where a single letter was intended) or to wasted resources (two requests for recovery of data when only one was desired). Longer delays can lead to user frustration.

Most frustrating of all are delays of random duration. One moment the user receives almost instantaneous service and the next moment the user must wait for what seems to be an eternity. Variable delays are generally the result of variations in load. Instant response is available when a single user is present, but delays become noticeable as more users attempt simultaneous use of system resources. In a well-designed system, loading effects should not be perceptible for rapid sequential operations (such as typing the separate letters of a name) and should be minimal for major operations (such as the delay between initiating a title search and first seeing the results of that search). Response time for rapid sequential operations should always be shorter than the time it would take a touch-typist to repeat a missed key (about 0.1 to 0.2 seconds). Response time (time elapsed to the beginning of responses) for more lengthy instructions should be a small fraction of the time taken to specify the operation, and should never exceed about three seconds. Note that it is only necessary that the response *begin* within that time.

The Fallacy of Human Homogeneity

Finally, the battle may not be won even if a system provides excellent interactive prompting for a naïve user. The needs of a new user are rarely the same as the needs of an experienced user. Interactive prompts that are a necessity for a new user may be a frustrating waste of time for an experienced worker who is using the terminal extensively. As a further complication, the type of display device in a terminal may affect people's acceptance of instructions which are superfluous to their needs. The relatively slow output rate of a printing terminal, for example, can be particularly exasperating if most of the printing consists of instructions the user does not need. The same instructions on a video display might be perfectly acceptable since the rapid rate of display would outweigh the fact that some of the instructions were superfluous.

Figure 3. User capabilities usually change with time and experience.

Design of human-machine interactions must, in short, take into consideration the needs of the novice user (who will require aid at every step), the experienced occasional user (who will need minimal prompting), and the experienced user with a substantial workload (who will be mostly interested in rapid response and minimal hindrance in getting the job done). These three levels of experience are frequently telescoped in time for a given individual who sits down at a terminal as a novice and stands up (several hours later) as an accomplished user. The well-designed system must accommodate all of these levels of expertise by an appropriate mixture of optional paths, self-selected "help" sequences, and careful human engineering. The human engineering must, above all, minimize idiosyncratic forms of interactions that simplify the work of a computer programmer at the expense of the convenience of users.

Conclusion

This paper has concentrated on viewpoints rather than details of technique for two reasons. First, the physical design of systems is rapidly changing as new components become available. For example, a few years ago it would have been reasonable to list the advantages and disadvantages of making the application characteristics of a particular system hardware-resident rather than software-resident (e.g., a keyboard designed for a specific application *v.* a general keyboard with software prompts). Changes in types of memory and display devices available are now blurring such distinctions. In general, specific suggestions about system configurations simply do not "age" well in times of rapid technological change.

Second, our experience has shown that the real source of problems in most design efforts has been failure to identify clearly the goals and procedures that define the system. In the absence of clear goals, computer-design specialists must substitute their own view of what is intended or needed. To the extent that these specialists have specific experience in the practical problems of a given application, their views may lead to successful designs. To the extent that these specialists rely on the fallacies described here, the designs may be dramatically unsuccessful. As in any

Figure 4. System designers can rarely predict all of the problems likely to be seen in a given application.

change in work procedures, there is a need for direct, active input by those who have experienced the reality of the task environment. When the change in work procedures requires investments in time and money of the magnitude demanded by selection or development of computer systems, that need becomes crucial.

The fallacies of system design described here can be averted most easily by continual, careful cooperation between design specialists and those who are thoroughly familiar with the ultimate application of the system. More than in any other form of computer system design, systems that provide interactive terminals for occasional use by minimally trained persons demand careful design to insure that expected performance occurs under realistic conditions. Systems that make unrealistic demands on user training, memory, or ability will not be truly successful even though they may function under ideal conditions.

REFERENCE

1. Broadbent, Donald A. "The Magic Number Seven After Fifteen Years." *In* Alan Kennedy and Alan Wilkes, eds. *Studies in Long Term Memory*. New York, Wiley, 1975, pp. 3-18.

CHRISTINE L. BORGMAN
University of Texas at Dallas

NEAL K. KASKE
Manager, Research Department
OCLC, Inc.

Determining the Number of Terminals Required for an On-Line Catalog through Queueing Analysis of Catalog Traffic Data

Introduction

Many libraries are in the process of closing their card catalogs and replacing them with microform or on-line catalogs. This change in catalog format in turn requires several important changes in catalog generation and support: (1) all cataloging data must be recorded in machine-readable form; (2) different equipment must be used, e.g., terminals are needed instead of typewriters, and microform readers or computer terminals are needed instead of card catalog cabinets; (3) the sorting sequence must change from a manual filing-rules sequence to a machine-generated sorting sequence; (4) staff must be trained both in the procedures to create machine-readable records and in the use of the catalog format; and (5) patrons must be taught to use the new catalog format.

It is the change in equipment needed in libraries that is dealt with in this paper, specifically, determining the number of terminals required for an on-line catalog. The change in catalog access equipment, from card catalog cabinets to microform readers or computer terminals, means a major change in the method of access to the contents of the catalog. Currently, only one complete card catalog set is needed for normal catalog traffic in any one location. Since the card file is divided into many discrete access units (file drawers), patrons rarely have to wait for access to the desired section of the catalog, even at peak periods. With microform readers and terminals, however, the entire catalog is available through one single equipment item, and access is such that only one person at a time can enter the catalog through that piece of equipment. Therefore, multiple microform copies of the catalog or multiple terminals are required to serve multiple users.

To house the new catalog format, large equipment purchases are likely to be necessary. Thus, budgeting and planning become major management concerns. Sufficient equipment must be purchased to assure prompt user access, even during peak use periods. Yet, expensive terminals and readers should not sit idle for long intervals during slow use periods.

Background of the Study

In assessing equipment needs for the conversion to an on-line catalog, the Dallas Public Library initiated a study of current catalog use, with plans to incorporate the findings from the investigation into its design and planning process. This investigation was limited by the available data. The data collected on current card catalog use were analyzed and used to project equipment requirements for an on-line catalog. Usage levels and patterns for the new catalog were assumed identical to those of the present card catalog. While there will be significant changes in both level and patterns of catalog use with the implementation of an on-line catalog, until such changes can be quantified there is no way to incorporate them into the study.

Dallas Public Library is a large metropolitan library system with a central library and seventeen branches (plus an eighteenth under construction), with an annual circulation of 4 million items, and with holdings of 2.5 million volumes. The library has been automating its services, in stages, since 1971. When completed, the total automated system will include: an on-line, optical character recognition (OCR)-based circulation system that will post circulation status information to the on-line catalog; a library materials acquisition and accounting system; and a film-booking system. All program development and equipment support has been done by the City of Dallas Data Services Department. As of early 1980, the automated circulation system is operational with an on-line delinquent patron file, an on-line circulation statistics subsystem, and a batch transaction card check-out/check-in system. Much of the circulation system presently in use has been operational since 1973. The on-line catalog has been operational and publicly accessible with partial holdings since February 1978. The catalog contains fixed-length, non-MARC records of all central library monographic holdings, plus branch library holdings added since February 1978. Retrospective conversion of branch library holdings is expected to be complete in 1982.

The on-line catalog was made available to all library agencies in February 1978 through the circulation system terminals located behind circulation desks in all branches and the central library. When initially implemented, the on-line catalog could be searched by author, title, author/title combination, or call number (Dewey Decimal system). In late 1979, a subject search based on Library of Congress Classification subject headings was added. Starting in mid-1978, additional CRT terminals were provided in public service areas to be exclusively used for access to the on-line catalog. By early 1980, every Dallas Public Library branch had at least two terminals, one in the public service area and one in the workroom for retrospective conversion of holdings. Additional terminals for public service usage will be added throughout the 1980/81 and 1981/82 fiscal years.

The next major project will be completion of the circulation system, upgrading it to a full on-line system with a patron database and links to the on-line catalog, so that circulation status information can be posted to catalog records. The first stage in design of the acquisitions system has been completed, but no programming has yet been done on that system. The film-booking system will be the last project to be completed. The central library will move to a new, much larger downtown facility in 1982, and the on-line catalog and circulation system will be operational when the new building opens.[1]

Strategy of the Study

Early in the planning stages for the automated systems, the need for a fairly precise estimate of equipment requirements became apparent. The investigation was initiated by soliciting opinions from the public service librarians in the branch libraries and the central library. Their opinions showed great variance, so a scientific approach was sought.

Aware that other libraries had already made the conversion to microform and on-line catalogs, the study team decided to survey other libraries to learn the means used to determine the number of pieces of equipment required. We were not able to identify other public libraries that had already converted to on-line catalogs, so the survey was restricted to public libraries which had converted to microform catalogs. Because microform and on-line catalogs both require one station per concurrent user, we assumed that the quantity of equipment required for each would be the same. We were aware that there are qualitative differences between microform and on-line catalogs, but no data were available to indicate the effect that these differences would have on the number of stations required. We chose to make the assumption of equality, unless some useful data for distinguishing between microform and on-line equipment needs were later discovered.

For the purposes of a mail survey, lists of microform catalog users were obtained from microform catalog vendors. The survey was restricted to public libraries with microform catalogs. The results of the unpublished survey were inconclusive for the purpose of obtaining quantitative data on how the number of microform readers was determined. Libraries generally said the number was determined by "guesstimate," or by "buying as many as we could with the money available." One library stated, "the more we buy, the more they get used." The only quantitative formula given was one from a study done by Butler, West and Aveney.[2] A brief review of the project and formula are given by Aveney and Ghikas.[3]

As neither the informal internal survey nor the mail survey provided the needed data, the Dallas Public Library decided to do its own study. The study was based on card catalog usage systemwide, sampling both traffic at the catalogs and the duration of the search time at the catalogs. The library hoped to gather enough data to determine the number of terminals required both to maximize equipment usage and to minimize patron waiting time.

It was not practical to do a detailed traffic study at each of the library's catalogs. The Dallas Public Library has a large number of card catalogs. The central library has a union catalog for the library system, plus individual catalogs for each of four subject divisions. Each of the seventeen branches has at least one card catalog (combined adult and youth holdings); most have separate catalogs for adult and youth materials. Therefore, representative catalogs were chosen for the study, based on collection size and rate of circulation. The main union catalog was included in the study as it is unique in the system, and one of the four subject division catalogs was selected to represent those four catalogs. Branches were divided, by holdings and circulation, into three classes: large, medium and small. Two branches were selected from each of the three classes. The following catalogs were chosen for study:

Central Library:
  Central library main catalog: This is the union catalog for the Dallas Public Library system.
  History and Social Sciences catalog: This catalog contains records for the 109,000 volumes held by this division of the central library.

Large Branches:
  Audelia Road Branch catalogs: This branch holds 84,250 volumes and has an annual circulation of 345,000 items.
  Park Forest Branch catalogs: This branch holds 71,000 volumes and has an annual circulation of 304,750 items.

Medium Branches:
  Lakewood Branch catalogs: This branch holds 65,200 volumes and has an annual circulation of 247,750 items.

Hampton-Illinois Branch catalogs: This branch holds 66,000 volumes and has an annual circulation of 240,750 items.

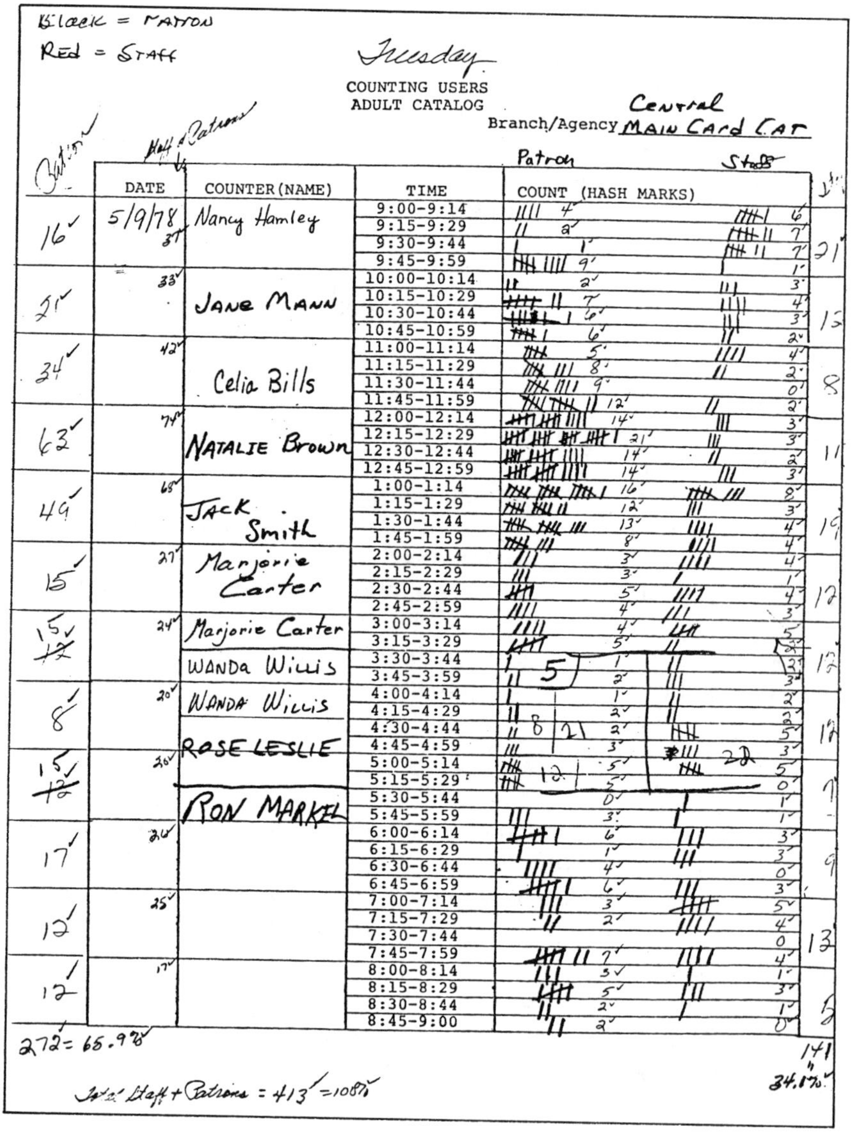

Black = Patron
Red = Staff

Tuesday

COUNTING USERS
ADULT CATALOG

Branch/Agency Central MAIN Card CAT

Patron	Half Patrons	DATE	COUNTER (NAME)	TIME	COUNT (HASH MARKS) Patron	Staff	Staff
16	37	5/9/78	Nancy Hamley	9:00-9:14	4	6	21
				9:15-9:29	2	7	
				9:30-9:44	1	7	
				9:45-9:59	9	1	
21	33		JANE MANN	10:00-10:14	2	3	12
				10:15-10:29	7	4	
				10:30-10:44	6	3	
				10:45-10:59	6	2	
34	42		Celia Bills	11:00-11:14	5	4	8
				11:15-11:29	8	2	
				11:30-11:44	9	0	
				11:45-11:59	12	2	
63	74		NATALIE Brown	12:00-12:14	14	3	11
				12:15-12:29	21	3	
				12:30-12:44	14	2	
				12:45-12:59	14	3	
49	68		JACK Smith	1:00-1:14	16	8	19
				1:15-1:29	12	3	
				1:30-1:44	13	4	
				1:45-1:59	8	4	
15	27		Marjorie Carter	2:00-2:14	3	4	12
				2:15-2:29	3	1	
				2:30-2:44	5	4	
				2:45-2:59	4	3	
15 (~~17~~)	24		Marjorie Carter	3:00-3:14	4	5	13
				3:15-3:29	5	2	
			WANDA Willis	3:30-3:44	1	3	
				3:45-3:59	2	3	
8	20		WANDA Willis	4:00-4:14	1	2	12
				4:15-4:29	2	2	
				4:30-4:44	2	5	
			ROSE LESLIE	4:45-4:59	3	3	
15 (~~12~~)	26			5:00-5:14	5	5	7
				5:15-5:29	5	0	
			RON MARKEL	5:30-5:44	0	1	
				5:45-5:59	3	1	
17	26			6:00-6:14	6	3	9
				6:15-6:29	1	3	
				6:30-6:44	4	0	
				6:45-6:59	6	3	
12	25			7:00-7:14	3	5	13
				7:15-7:29	2	4	
				7:30-7:44		0	
				7:45-7:59	7	4	
12	17			8:00-8:14	3	1	5
				8:15-8:29	5	3	
				8:30-8:44	2	1	
				8:45-9:00	2	0	

272 = 65.9%

141 = 34.1%

Total Staff + Patrons = 413 = 100%

Figure 1. Traffic at the Catalog

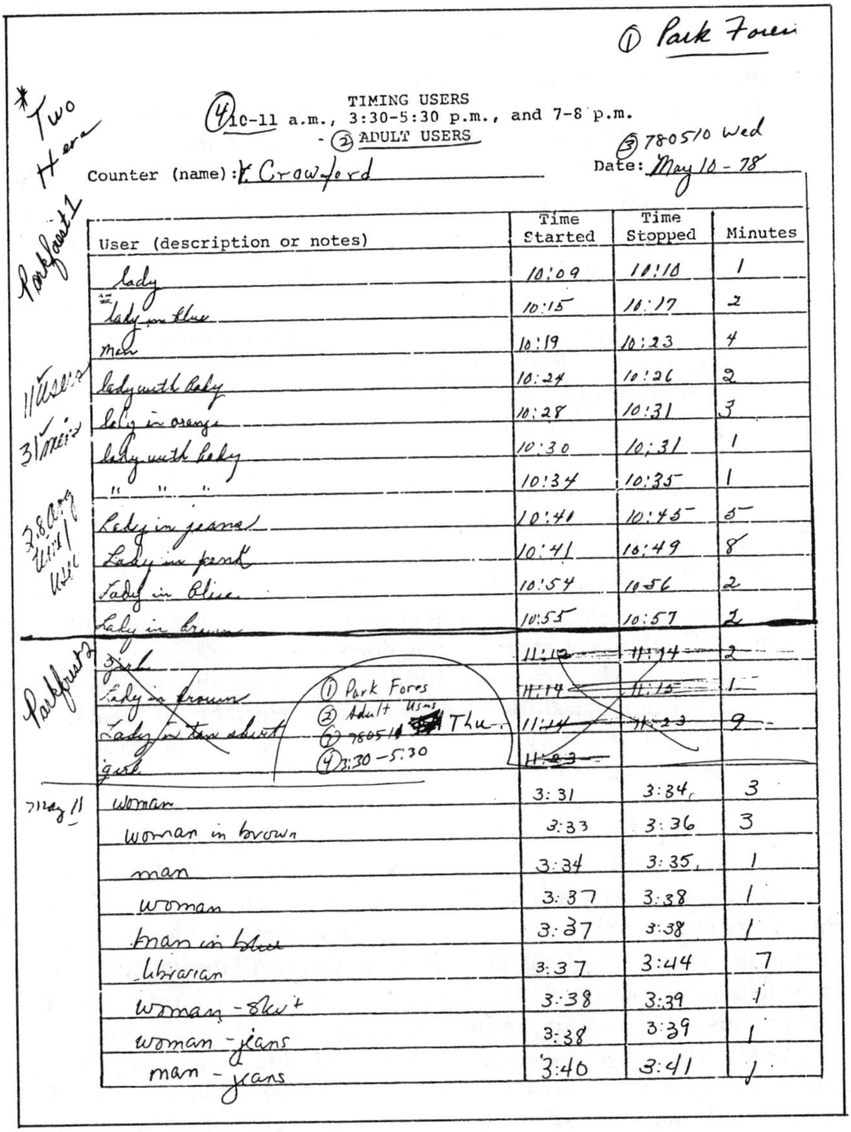
① Park Fores

TIMING USERS
④ 10-11 a.m., 3:30-5:30 p.m., and 7-8 p.m.
- ② ADULT USERS

③ 780510 Wed

Counter (name): V. Crawford

Date: May 10 - 78

User (description or notes)	Time Started	Time Stopped	Minutes
lady	10:09	10:10	1
lady in blue	10:15	10:17	2
man	10:19	10:23	4
lady with baby	10:24	10:26	2
lady in orange	10:28	10:31	3
lady with baby	10:30	10:31	1
" " "	10:34	10:35	1
Lady in jeans	10:41	10:45	5
Lady in pink	10:41	10:49	8
Lady in blue	10:54	10:56	2
Lady in brown	10:55	10:57	2
girl	11:10	11:14	2
Lady in brown	11:14	11:15	1
Lady in tan skirt	11:14	11:23	9
girl	11:23		
woman	3:31	3:34	3
woman in brown	3:33	3:36	3
man	3:34	3:35	1
woman	3:37	3:38	1
man in blue	3:37	3:38	1
librarian	3:37	3:44	7
woman - skirt	3:38	3:39	1
woman - jeans	3:38	3:39	1
man - jeans	3:40	3:41	1

① Park Fores
② Adult Users
③ 780511 Thu
④ 3:30-5:30

Figure 2. Duration of Search Time

Small Branches:

Lancaster-Kiest Branch catalogs: This branch holds 65,900 volumes and has an annual circulation of 70,630 items.

Oaklawn Branch catalogs: This branch holds 29,500 volumes and has an annual circulation of 97,000 items.

The data were collected during one week in May 1978. Two different types of data—traffic at the catalog and duration of search time—were tracked on two different sets of data collection forms (see figs. 1 and 2).

Traffic at the catalog. Records were kept of how many people used the catalog, by 15-minute periods of the day. Data were collected for "one day" during the week: a full morning, full afternoon, and full evening were covered during the week, although not all fell on the same day. One complete Saturday also was covered. Breaking up the day this way was necessary, as only the central library is actually open morning, afternoon and evening on a single day. Central library hours are 9 A.M.—9 P.M. Monday through Friday, and 9 A.M.—6 P.M. Saturday. Branches are open 10 A.M.—6 P.M. some weekdays and 12 P.M.—9 P.M. on others, plus 10 A.M.—6 P.M. on Saturday. Breaking up the day in segments also simplified the scheduling of personnel to do the data collection.

Duration of search time. Three periods of the day were selected for this part of the study: 10 A.M.—11 A.M. (slow period), 3:30 P.M.—5:30 P.M. (peak period), and 7 P.M.—8 P.M. (peak period). During these three time periods, each person going to the catalog was clocked in and clocked out. This was done by jotting down brief descriptive notes about the person on the data collection form to keep track of all individuals using the catalog.

The data from each study were further subdivided by patron and staff usage at the central library (both the main catalog and the History and Social Sciences catalog) and by adult and youth catalog usage at the branch libraries. The latter subdivision was necessary as some of the branches have separate catalogs for adult and youth holdings. The division was made by catalog, rather than by individual; that is, a patron at the youth catalog was considered "youth" regardless of the person's age. The division by patron and staff was at the request of the central library staff, and was kept for its own usage. Because the total data collection was small for staff and youth, those data were not aggregated. Day of the week, time of day, and location distinctions were made in the final data analysis.

Data collection was done both by Dallas Public Library staff and by library volunteers. A total of over 200 individuals were involved in the data collection. Library volunteers were very cooperative and some helped in different agencies from those in which they normally volunteered. We emphasized the fact that data would be extrapolated to represent the entire Dallas Public Library system, so that assistance given at any agency would benefit other agencies within the library system.

The data were manually tabulated by the library staff, showing patterns of usage and averages by time of day. Some correction to the data on number of staff inquiries was made for the central main card catalog, based on usage of the on-line catalog terminal. At the time of the study, that was the only location that provided readily available access to the on-line catalog. No similar corrections were made in the branch library data collection.

The original intent of the study was to do further data analysis using queueing theory. It was found that the data manipulation required was too complex to perform manually, and that City of Dallas computer time was not readily available for the task. Copies of all of the raw data collection sheets, therefore, were provided to Neal Kaske of the OCLC, Inc., Research Department in June 1979 for analysis by computer, using queueing algorithms. The analysis which follows is a result of the work done at OCLC.

Data Analysis

The OCLC Research Department used a multiserver queueing model to analyze the data collected by the Dallas Public Library. This model assumes a common stream of patron traffic, a finite number of identical servers (terminals or readers), a common waiting line when all servers are busy, and a "first-in, first-out" selection from the waiting line. The particular multiserver model used was adapted from a model documented in the IBM publication, *Analysis of Some Queueing Models in Real-Time Systems.*[4] A graphic representation of this multiserver queue is shown in figure 3.

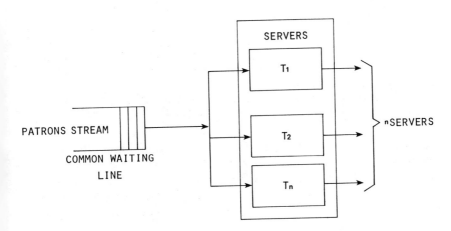

Figure 3. Model of Multiserver Queue

The first step of data analysis was to convert the tallies from the "Duration of Search Time" forms (fig. 2) to machine-readable format. Only complete data records (containing both a starting and ending time) were converted. Computer programs were then written to process these records and calculate the following values:

mean service time (T_s)
mean interarrival time (T_a)
traffic intensity (T_i)

Traffic intensity is defined as

$$T_i = \frac{T_s}{T_a}$$

and represents the amount of system capacity in demand at any given time. The records were processed in sets by location, date and time of day. Then, a traffic intensity (T_i) value was calculated for each set.

Once traffic intensity was calculated, the data were tested to determine if they fit a Poisson distribution. If the data did fit the Poisson distribution (which they did when analyzed by hour blocks of catalog use), standard queueing formulas could be used to calculate the mean waiting line and time for a given number of servers at low, average and peak catalog use. Tables 1 and 2 report traffic intensity values and traffic parameters for these three levels of catalog use. The parameters computed were: (1) the probability that a patron will find a reader/terminal idle; (2) the mean length of the line of patrons waiting to use a reader/terminal; and (3) the mean time a patron will need to wait in line for a reader/terminal. Each of the parameters was calculated for one to eight servers for the catalog.

To make the data useful for Dallas Public Library management, a set of decision rules was established for use with the data. The decision rules were: (1) the patron must find a terminal/reader available 90 percent of the time; (2) there must be no waiting line for a terminal (on average less than one patron in line at any given time); and (3) the patron must wait in line thirty seconds or less. The effects of these decision rules are shown in table 3.

To enhance the usefulness of the data for library management, a sensitivity analysis was conducted. The sensitivity analysis provided a range of values for the measure of congestion (traffic intensity). For the analysis, the derived values for traffic intensity were doubled and halved, and the same three decision rules were applied to the values. The results for doubled and halved values are shown in tables 4 and 5, respectively. The problem of determining the number of terminals required is thus bounded.

TABLE 1
TRAFFIC INTENSITY VALUES AND TRAFFIC PARAMETERS—CENTRAL LIBRARY

Central Library	Time	Date May 1978	Traffic Intensity		Number of Servers							
					1	2	3	4	5	6	7	8
History and Social Sciences												
Peak	10:00-11:00 A.M.	6	1.03	P	i	0.65	0.89	0.98	1.00	1.00	1.00	1.00
				L	i	2.26	0.34	0.05	0.01	0.00	0.00	0.00
				W	i	13.55	2.01	0.29	0.04	0.01	0.00	0.00
Low	3:30-5:30 P.M.	9	0.08	P	0.92	1.00	1.00	1.00	1.00	1.00	1.00	1.00
				L	0.10	0.00	0.00	0.00	0.00	0.00	0.00	0.00
				W	1.38	0.03	0.00	0.00	0.00	0.00	0.00	0.00
Average	(N=43)		0.34	P	0.66	0.94	0.99	1.00	1.00	1.00	1.00	1.00
				L	1.37	0.10	0.01	0.00	0.00	0.00	0.00	0.00
				W	10.48	0.74	0.04	0.00	0.00	0.00	0.00	0.00
Main Catalog												
Peak	3:30-5:30 P.M.	6	3.35	P	i	i	i	0.33	0.67	0.85	0.94	0.98
				L	i	i	i	6.63	1.31	0.37	0.11	0.03
				W	i	i	i	12.81	2.53	0.72	0.22	0.06
Low	10:00-11:00 A.M.	6	1.05	P	i	0.64	0.89	0.98	1.00	1.00	1.00	1.00
				L	i	1.20	0.18	0.03	0.00	0.00	0.00	0.00
				W	i	3.52	0.52	0.08	0.01	0.00	0.00	0.00
Average	(N=182)		2.17	P	i	i	0.47	0.78	0.92	0.97	0.99	1.00
				L	i	i	3.00	0.58	0.14	0.03	0.01	0.00
				W	i	i	6.51	1.25	0.29	0.07	0.02	0.00

P=the probability that a patron will find a reader/terminal idle
L=the mean length of the line of patrons waiting to use a reader/terminal
W=the mean time (in fractional minutes) a patron will need to wait in line for a reader/terminal
i=infinite

TABLE 2
TRAFFIC INTENSITY VALUES AND TRAFFIC PARAMETERS—BRANCH LIBRARIES

Branch Libraries	Time	Date May 1978	Traffic Intensity		Number of Servers							
					1	2	3	4	5	6	7	8
Audelia Road												
Peak	3:30-5:30 P.M.	8	2.67	P	—	—	0.20	0.61	0.84	0.94	0.98	0.99
				L	—	—	9.75	1.16	0.28	0.08	0.02	0.01
				W	—	—	14.49	1.73	0.42	0.11	0.03	0.01
Low	10:00-11:00 A.M.	8	0.44	P	0.56	0.90	0.99	1.00	1.00	1.00	1.00	1.00
				L	1.73	0.14	0.01	0.00	0.00	0.00	0.00	0.00
				W	8.64	0.70	0.05	0.00	0.00	0.00	0.00	0.00
Average (N=241)			1.78	P	—	0.16	0.63	0.87	0.96	0.99	1.00	1.00
				L	—	10.94	0.87	0.17	0.04	0.01	0.00	0.00
				W	—	17.88	1.42	0.27	0.06	0.01	0.00	0.00
Park Forest												
Peak	3:30-5:30 P.M.	11	1.45	P	—	0.39	0.77	0.93	0.98	1.00	1.00	1.00
				L	—	2.54	0.35	0.06	0.01	0.00	0.00	0.00
				W	—	4.02	0.55	0.10	0.02	0.00	0.00	0.00
Low	10:00-11:00 A.M.	13	0.38	P	0.62	0.93	0.99	1.00	1.00	1.00	1.00	1.00
				L	0.67	0.05	0.00	0.00	0.00	0.00	0.00	0.00
				W	1.95	0.15	0.01	0.00	0.00	0.00	0.00	0.00
Average (N=204)			0.94	P	0.06	0.64	0.91	0.98	1.00	1.00	1.00	1.00
				L	28.36	0.63	0.08	0.01	0.00	0.00	0.00	0.00
				W	55.47	1.23	0.15	0.02	0.00	0.00	0.00	0.00
Hampton-Illinois												
Peak	10:00-11:00 A.M.	13	1.31	P	—	0.48	0.81	0.95	0.99	1.00	1.00	1.00
				L	—	1.84	0.27	0.05	0.01	0.00	0.00	0.00
				W	—	3.45	0.51	0.09	0.01	0.00	0.00	0.00
Low	10:00-11:00 A.M.	10	0.53	P	0.47	0.86	0.98	1.00	1.00	1.00	1.00	1.00
				L	2.63	0.22	0.02	0.00	0.00	0.00	0.00	0.00
				W	11.40	0.96	0.08	0.01	0.00	0.00	0.00	0.00
Average (N=163)			1.10	P	—	0.61	0.88	0.97	0.99	1.00	1.00	1.00
				L	—	1.02	0.15	0.02	0.00	0.00	0.00	0.00
				W	—	2.15	0.32	0.05	0.01	0.00	0.00	0.00

Location	Time			Stat	1	2	3	4	5	6	7	8
Lakewood												
Peak	10:00-11:00 A.M.	13	1.47	P	i	0.38	0.76	0.93	0.98	1.00	1.00	1.00
				L	i	3.78	0.51	0.09	0.02	0.00	0.00	0.00
				W	i	8.34	1.13	0.20	0.04	0.01	0.00	0.00
Low	10:00-11:00 A.M.	9	0.42	P	0.58	0.91	0.99	1.00	1.00	1.00	1.00	1.00
				L	1.36	0.11	0.01	0.00	0.00	0.00	0.00	0.00
				W	6.03	0.48	0.03	0.00	0.00	0.00	0.00	0.00
Average	(N=145)		0.79	P	0.21	0.72	0.94	0.99	1.00	1.00	1.00	1.00
				L	9.13	0.55	0.06	0.01	0.00	0.00	0.00	0.00
				W	27.29	1.64	0.18	0.02	0.00	0.00	0.00	0.00
Lancaster-Kiest												
Peak	7:00-8:00 P.M.	9	1.63	P	i	0.27	0.69	0.90	0.97	0.99	1.00	1.00
				L	i	14.01	1.56	0.29	0.06	0.01	0.00	0.00
				W	i	60.05	6.70	1.26	0.25	0.05	0.01	0.00
Low	10:00-11:00 A.M.	13	0.31	P	0.69	0.95	1.00	1.00	1.00	1.00	1.00	1.00
				L	0.71	0.05	0.00	0.00	0.00	0.00	0.00	0.00
				W	3.69	0.24	0.01	0.00	0.00	0.00	0.00	0.00
Average	(N=67)		0.57	P	0.43	0.84	0.98	1.00	1.00	1.00	1.00	1.00
				L	4.10	0.34	0.03	0.00	0.00	0.00	0.00	0.00
				W	22.35	1.87	0.16	0.01	0.00	0.00	0.00	0.00
Oaklawn												
Peak	3:30-5:30 P.M.	13	0.97	P	0.03	0.62	0.91	0.98	1.00	1.00	1.00	1.00
				L	98.12	1.08	0.13	0.02	0.00	0.00	0.00	0.00
				W	291.72	3.20	0.39	0.05	0.01	0.00	0.00	0.00
Low	7:00-8:00 P.M.	9	0.12	P	0.88	0.99	1.00	1.00	1.00	1.00	1.00	1.00
				L	0.15	0.00	0.00	0.00	0.00	0.00	0.00	0.00
				W	1.54	0.04	0.00	0.00	0.00	0.00	0.00	0.00
Average	(N=71)		0.41	P	0.59	0.91	0.99	1.00	1.00	1.00	1.00	1.00
				L	1.52	0.12	0.01	0.00	0.00	0.00	0.00	0.00
				W	8.08	0.63	0.04	0.00	0.00	0.00	0.00	0.00

P=the probability that a patron will find a reader/terminal idle
L=the mean length of the line of patrons waiting to use a reader/terminal
W=the mean time (in fractional minutes) a patron will need to wait in line for a reader/terminal
i=infinite

TABLE 3
DECISION TABLE SHOWING EFFECTS OF DECISION RULES

	To assure patron will find a terminal/reader free 90% of the time		Number of Servers Needed — To assure fewer than one user in line at any given time		To assure users wait in line ½-minute or less	
	Peak	Average	Peak	Average	Peak	Average
Large Branches						
Audelia Road	6	5	5	3	5	4
Park Forest	4	3	3	2	4	3
Medium Branches						
Hampton-Illinois	4	4	3	3	4	3
Lakewood	4	3	3	2	4	3
Small Branches						
Lancaster-Kiest	4	3	4	2	5	3
Oaklawn	3	2	3	2	3	2
Central Library						
Main Catalog	7	5	6	4	6	5
History & Social Sciences	4	2	3	2	4	3

TABLE 4
DECISION TABLE FOR TRAFFIC INTENSITY DOUBLED

| | Number of Servers Needed | | | | | |
| | To assure patron will find a terminal/reader free 90% of the time | | To assure fewer than one user in line at any given time | | To assure users wait in line ½-minute or less | |
	Peak	Average	Peak	Average	Peak	Average
Large Branches						
Audelia Road	10	7	7	5	8	6
Park Forest	6	5	3	2	5	4
Medium Branches						
Hampton-Illinois	6	5	4	4	5	5
Lakewood	6	4	5	3	6	4
Small Branches						
Lancaster-Kiest	7	4	6	3	7	4
Oaklawn	5	3	4	2	5	3
Central Library						
Main Catalog	11	8	9	7	11	8
History & Social Sciences	5	3	4	2	6	3

TABLE 5
DECISION TABLE FOR TRAFFIC INTENSITY REDUCED BY HALF

| | Number of Servers Needed | | | | | |
| | To assure patron will find a terminal/reader free 90% of the time | | To assure fewer than one user in line at any given time | | To assure users wait in line ½-minute or less | |
	Peak	Average	Peak	Average	Peak	Average
Large Branches						
Audelia Road	4	3	3	2	4	3
Park Forest	3	3	2	2	3	2
Medium Branches						
Hampton-Illinois	3	3	2	2	3	3
Lakewood	3	2	2	2	3	2
Small Branches						
Lancaster-Kiest	3	2	3	2	2	2
Oaklawn	3	2	2	1	3	2
Central Library						
Main Catalog	5	4	4	3	5	4
History & Social Sciences	3	2	2	1	3	2

Summary

The data collected for this study represented actual usage levels and patterns for specific agencies of the Dallas Public Library system. The data analysis determined how many terminals were required to support the same levels and patterns of usage for the on-line catalog that were evident for the card catalog. There are two limitations to this study:

1. The results of the data analysis are specifically applicable to the Dallas Public Library; a direct extrapolation of the data to other libraries, based on figures such as circulation, traffic, and holdings, may not be legitimate.
2. The usage of an on-line catalog will not be the same as the usage of a card catalog. On-line catalogs are not limited to all terminals being in one location, in the manner that all drawers of a card catalog must be in one location. Therefore, terminals may be scattered throughout the library, or in other buildings. More or less time per search may be required for the catalog with an on-line terminal. The card catalog (with the exception of the central library main catalog) contains records only for the library agency in which it is located; the on-line catalog, however, will be a union catalog for the library system, which will affect usage patterns. If printers are available for the terminals, users will print out the desired records rather than spending time at the catalog copying them. These changes in usage patterns are only the ones that are now anticipated, and it is expected that other changes will occur.

While the limitations to the study are significant, it is still a quantitative step forward. The early investigations showed that libraries have been guessing at the amount of equipment needed, without having any quantitative figures to support their guesses. The figures for terminal requirements obtained from this study provide a starting point for equipment purchase. Adjustments can be made from this point based on actual usage. The data obtained from the study show that in most cases, fewer terminals are required than were originally thought. In one case, there may be as many as five fewer terminals required to meet peak usage than the Dallas Public Library staff had originally estimated.

The Dallas Public Library is using this study to support the budget request for terminals in support of the on-line catalog. The library considers the results to be useful management information, and planning decisions will be made accordingly.[5]

REFERENCES

1. Christine L. Borgman was Systems Analyst at Dallas Public Library at the time this study was performed, and conducted the study in that capacity. *See* Borgman, Christine L. "Library Automation Development at Dallas Public Library." *In* Bernard M. Fry and Clayton A. Shepherd, comps. *Information Management in the 1980's: Proceedings of the ASIS Annual Meeting.* Vol. 14. White Plains, N.Y., Knowledge Industry, 1977, fiche 2, pp. A9-14; _____ . "The Role of Technology for the Dallas Public Library in Long Range Planning" (paper presented at the Dallas Public Library Long Range Planning Retreat, Waxahachie, Tex., May 12-14, 1977). (ED 153 698)

2. Butler, Brett, et al. *Library and Patron Response to the COM Catalog: Use and Evaluation.* Los Altos, Calif., Information Access, 1978.

3. Aveney, Brian, and Ghikas, Mary F. "Reactions Measured: 600 Users Meet the COM Catalog," *American Libraries* 10:82-83, Feb. 1979.

4. *Analysis of Some Queueing Models in Real-Time Systems* (IBM Data Processing Techniques, GF20-0007-1). 2d ed., White Plains, N.Y., IBM, 1971.

5. William Slaughter (Associate Director for Management Services, Dallas Public Library), to Borgman and Kaske, May 9, 1980.

MARGARET BECKMAN
Chief Librarian
University of Guelph
Guelph, Ontario

Public Access at the University of Guelph Library

Introduction

The University of Guelph is one of fifteen provincially assisted universities in Ontario. Guelph is a medium-sized institution with 10,000 students (1000 of whom are graduate), approximately sixty miles northwest of Toronto. Although it received its charter in 1964, the university was based on the integration of three existing agricultural and veterinary colleges which date to the middle of the last century.

This changed university status and the formation of four new colleges led to the need for immediate acquisition of thousands of monographs, documents and serials. Automated cataloging systems were seen as the only solution to the organization, access and processing problems which resulted. By 1967 the University of Guelph Library staff had designed and implemented separate automated systems for the cataloging and processing of government publications, monographs and serials, and a retrospective conversion of the original college catalogs was completed by 1968.

The central library building on the Guelph campus, the McLaughlin Library, which opened in 1968, now houses 1.5 million volumes in 270,000 square feet. One of the design criteria for the building was automated circulation control, so that automated circulation became an important subset of the Guelph cataloging system, extracting necessary data elements from the Guelph master file of bibliographic records.

Previous Batch Circulation System

This basic circulation system, using punched book cards and patron badges, served Guelph reasonably well from 1968 until 1976; circulation transaction lists were printed daily, and overdue and fine notices, error and edit checklists, and management reports were produced as required. A simple system to handle reserve book circulation was added in 1973. The data collection terminals were changed in 1972 from IBM 1030s to Colorado Instruments (later Mohawk) C-DEKs, but the original concept of the system was not altered.

Reasons for the Change From Off-line to On-line System

By 1976 the pressure on the library was considerably greater with 10,000 students than it had been when the building opened for 3000 students in 1968. For instance, in 1976-77 some 500,000 books and documents circulated, while in-library use was double that amount. In addition, the climate of economic restraint that influenced Ontario universities demanded strategies that would reduce or at least hold constant the existing library positions. Knowledge of changing technology led to consideration of an on-line circulation system early in 1976, and a study was mounted to identify specific problems or inadequacies of the existing batch circulation system, and to specify design requirements for a new on-line system. The following inadequacies were identified.

Mechanical breakdown. As a result of the transaction load mentioned above, the percentage of errors present in the circulation system increased greatly during 1975 and 1976. This was primarily due to mechanical breakdowns in the C-DEK terminals, which were no longer being manufactured or supported by Mohawk. Each incident of terminal breakdown increased the possibility of incorrect data being recorded.

Errors. The C-DEK terminal used a very unsophisticated method to prevent the acceptance of incorrect data (double punch and blank column detection), allowing errors to creep into the system without detection. Staff errors also contributed to mistakes in the overdue and fine notices produced by the circulation system, creating unnecessary friction between library staff and users. In addition, students in increasing numbers had discovered ways to subvert the system, complicating the errors which the breakdowns and staff were causing.

In constrast, current technology for data collection uses bar-coded labels, with an error potential of one in 200,000 reads. This rate can be further reduced by a 10 percent chance of the error matching a correct record; thus, the net theoretical error possibility is one in 2 million. It was felt that adoption of such a system at Guelph would not only eliminate errors but would also stop the subverting of the system by patrons, since the labels are manufactured in such a way that any attempt to remove them results in their destruction.

Cost and inefficiency. The library circulation staff had developed a series of checks and counter-checks to compensate for errors present in the off-line system. These checks were very time-consuming and expensive, and put an unnecessary load on an already overburdened staff. The cost of this checking was estimated at $13,500 annually.

Another area in which inefficiencies were evident was the library's holds procedure. This is one of the most critical procedures performed in the library, requiring manual checking of approximately 1 million books reshelved each year. This checking was done for the most part by student pages, and the fact that they were part-time and that so many persons were involved magnified the chances for error. Hold requests increased by an average of 50 percent per year from 1972, averaging 4000 requests in the fall and winter semesters of 1975/76.

It was concluded that an on-line system would eliminate the necessity for this manual checking routine at a savings of over $9000 in staff time annually. In addition, another area of user dissatisfaction would be removed, since the capture of items requested by patrons would be facilitated at the circulation point, before books reached the shelves or were charged from the library.

Reserve desk. Use of the reserve book system had increased almost 30 percent per year from the time the library opened in 1968, stretching the capacity of the simple semi-automated system to its limits. It was realized that a more sophisticated system was necessary, not only to maintain efficient service to the students without adding staff, but also to provide the management information necessary to ensure that the reserve service was being responsive to the needs of the teaching program.

In summary, the study concluded that benefits from conversion to an on-line circulation system would occur primarily in three areas: data accuracy, human error reduction, and more effective use of staff.

Design Criteria

In establishing the design criteria for an on-line circulation system, the University of Guelph Library looked beyond the basic functional requirements of circulation. We envisaged the capability of a single library system, albeit consisting of not necessarily compatible units, with direct access by staff and users alike. We also wanted a system which would have adequate backup procedures and be responsive, at minimum cost, to changing requirements within our own library system.

Based on the early experience with our first circulation system, we emphasized the importance of the relationship between the circulation system and the catalog. The continuance of that relationship was considered of primary importance, which meant that the circulation records should be a subset of the catalog data base in the Guelph system.

Our previous involvement with a bibliographic utility-centered system, the University of Toronto Library Automation System (UTLAS), also influenced the design criteria. For two years we had participated in the on-line cataloging system at UTLAS, with our catalog records stored on the central system in Toronto. We had found ourselves locked into an inflexible system that responded to needs perceived to be common to the group, but not necessarily meeting specific requirements of the individual library. Discussions of on-line circulation and acquisition systems linked to the central cataloging system but able to respond adequately to local needs and policies were not encouraged. After two years of expensive and frustrating experience, we returned to our in-house systems, determined to remain independent for local processing and to purchase needed bibliographic data from utilities if and when necessary. These philosophical design requirements may be expressed in greater detail. The system must:

1. operate on an in-house minicomputer with adequate backup procedures to ensure continuous operation;
2. provide capability for direct use by the students and faculty, minimizing the involvement of library staff in routine inquiry procedures;
3. provide capability for on-line catalog inquiry as part of the circulation system;
4. be able to interface with other components of the library system, providing an integrated and responsive total library operation; and
5. provide capability for linking with on-line circulation systems and/or catalogs operating in other Ontario university libraries.

These five requirements were most influential in making the final selection of an appropriate system, since no existing on-line circulation system seemed to encompass either the philosophy or power which the Guelph requirements demanded. Essential would be a minicomputer capable of sorting and processing all Guelph files of machine-readable records, irrespective of record format or file size. In 1977 the Guelph library files included:

monographs, including audiovisual materials (films, tapes, etc.) cataloged in a MARC-compatible format—400,000 records;
government publications coded using the Guelph Documentation System, which assigns each document a unique, jurisdiction-based document number—270,000 records;
maps coded in a locally designed system with a geographic map number—50,000 records;
serials which do not circulate but which are wanted for display in any

catalog inquiry system. Guelph serials are classified by the Library of Congress system, and individual issue holdings would need to be displayed for inquiry and management information purposes— 10,000 records.

In addition, capability for storing MARC files on-line was considered a requirement for both cataloging and acquisitions functions, and assumed a high priority.

With all design criteria included in a specification document, we received tenders from a variety of vendors. We chose a joint development proposal from a Canadian company, GEAC, because it most closely met our design criteria and would allow us to implement our system philosophy. We felt strongly that a system designed with the involvement of Guelph library staff would allow modifications and changes by that staff with relatively little difficulty, particularly since minicomputer technology was involved. We also felt that without an integrated on-line system, we could not make the anticipated staff reductions without reducing direct services to the user.

System Design

File Design

Although an efficient on-line circulation system was the primary objective of the design phase, the need for coordination with the cataloging acquisition, serials, and documents systems was an essential aspect of the Guelph design philosophy. For this reason, the design phase began with a study of file structures in bibliographic processing systems in use elsewhere in North America or Europe. Without hindering the circulation function, we hoped to be able to provide integrated access to all the Guelph records in their varying formats, without the necessity of actual conversion to a common record structure.

This objective was met by adopting a method for structuring the files for internal processing similar to that of the DOBIS system, implemented at Dortmund, West Germany, in 1976. This concept disperses the various data elements of each record to different files, and links them with keys, pointers and/or indexes. Thus, personal names from the monograph file, which has a MARC-like structure, are held in the same file as personal names from the Guelph document file, with its simple documentation structure. When displayed on the terminal, names from both files are shown together. If a user or staff member wants to see a complete record, a simple instruction pulls the record together. The call number or document number related to a name (or title, or other data element) reveals to the user whether he is looking at a record for a monograph, document, etc. It should be apparent that an authority system is inherent in the system, precluding the expensive necessity of creating and maintaining a separate one.

Public Inquiry
The second key criterion in the system design was that of public inquiry or use of the system. University of Guelph Library experience with retrieval systems such as CAN/OLE (Canadian On-Line Enquiry), Lockheed and SDC (System Development Corp.) had indicated that the staff's role as intermediaries was a necessary part of the service. It was agreed that a circulation system which depended on library staff to interpret or assist in access to the Guelph data bases for monographs, serials, documents, and maps, or to files of circulation and reserve system transaction information, would not be appropriate in an environment of financial restraint.

The inquiry module of the circulation system was designed, therefore, with self-instructing display screens which lead naturally or sequentially from one command, instruction or question to another. Each set of functions is displayed as a "menu" from which the user selects the key desired. After locating a wanted title (book or document), the user can move to another set of functions which allows him to determine the location, status and/or loan period for the book, and to place a hold on it if it is in circulation. He may also inquire about his own borrowing record— whether he has books out, when they are due, amount of fines (if any owing), etc.

If the student or faculty member becomes confused at any point in his use of the inquiry terminal, a simple action returns him to the first "menu" or display, which begins the step-by-step instructions again. The actual user functions are described in more detail later.

Operating System
The GEAC 8000 operating system facilitates the processing of bibliographic information by allowing complete variability of field and record structures. All fields in the records are bit-aligned, which means that only that number of bits required to store a particular data element is used. This fact, coupled with the use of advanced data compression techniques, allows not only efficient data storage but also high performance on the terminals. A very rapid response, which is essential for on-line inquiry, is possible because the volume of data transferred in a "mini" is much less than in conventional main-frame computer systems.

Further efficiencies are achieved through the file structure, where only as much data as are necessary to differentiate records are stored in any index entry. The data base management system of the GEAC also contributes to the essential efficiency of a public on-line system. All data in the system are stored in what GEAC defines as wrapped files. The data definition for each field is stored in what is called a wrapped table. This technique provides an additional level of data security in that a file in the wrapped state cannot be used on any other computer. Data would appear in this instance as a long string of bits. This technique further assists in data management in that a field can be modified in size or changed in definition simply by changing the tables in the field's wrapped table. The next time the file is updated, the change will have been accomplished.

UGLI, the GEAC processing language, is not only a language but also has facilities within it to provide for data base management and the application processers. There are two different operational levels, one for staff and one for patrons. The patron may query the system and perform certain functions, but cannot add data. The staff member may query the system and add or modify data as well as process them.

The maintenance processers produce and accept tapes, provide definitions, create and modify data, and reorganize files. The system creates new records but does not discard old records.

Description of User Menus
Each terminal in the system offers a selection of functions which can be performed. These are displayed on the CRT in a "menu." The command format is a numeric one, and the display itself indicates to the user how to select a desired function from the menu and how to proceed with each subsequent step or procedure.

System Operation, 1977-80

User Reaction
The system just described became operational in September 1977, after two months of parallel testing. We began with twenty-six terminals, including six available for public use. The first semester of use was a traumatic experience, for three reasons.

1. We operated without a fail-soft mechanism, i.e., a backup computer, and experienced a variety of problems. For example, a major thunderstorm knocked out our power supply. As a result, we installed a separate power feed.
2. Policies or regulations that we had built into the system, such as refusal to lend a book if a user owed more than a $5 fine, proved too inflexible on weekends since no staff could collect the money. We had to program in a series of overrides to compensate for hours when only student assistants were on duty.

3. We did not anticipate the enthusiastic response to the public terminals, as students happily abandoned the card catalog and lined up at the six public terminals.

In January 1978 our main computer, the GEAC 8000, arrived, and we transferred our existing library computer, a GEAC 800 on which we had implemented the system, to the fail-soft position. We also switched data input for all other library systems to the new GEAC 8000, so that the 800 was always available as a backup for circulation. This meant that changes could be made to the main system as development of enhancements or new modules continued, with no impact on the public circulation functions.

The positive user reaction cannot be overemphasized. Aside from including the on-line inquiry system in the regular library orientation program, as well as a brochure and publicity campaign, no special training was given. We depended on the display to instruct the students, and this proved quite successful. The terminals are located near reader service desks, so that during most hours the library is open, staff are available if a student is having difficulty "wanding" his badge.

Admittedly, we had a less enthusiastic response from many faculty members, who were resistant to "computers" as a matter of principle. We invited all faculty to come to special seminars, either individually or in department groups, and we volunteered to go to department meetings with a portable terminal. The ease and simplicity of the system soon converted most opponents, and we have had to do few individual faculty sessions.

Changes and Improvements

One of the first things discovered during the initial hectic semester in fall 1977 was that students, in particular, learned how to manipulate the system very quickly, and grew impatient with the screen sequence. By the beginning of the winter semester 1978, concurrent with the switch to the GEAC 8000, we had developed "Version II" of the system. Primarily, this allows the knowledgeable user to page more quickly through the menus, going directly to the function sought. We also added additional "INFORM" messages, so that more than 100 informational messages could be received via the terminal. We improved the filing arrangement, changed the display of the call number, and responded to other consistent user suggestions for the public inquiry mode.

In addition to doubling the number of terminals available for public access in the library, we decentralized access in fall 1979 by linking the GEAC 8000 to the campus Gandalf network. This made the on-line inquiry system available on any of the standard ASCII terminals on campus, allowing a read-only capability of accessing the library file. Response to this option, which we call "remote access," has also been enthusiastic. In addition, it creates many more potential services, such as remote placing of holds or inputting purchase requests. These functions await further testing of the remote-access module, and the development of adequate security for remote entry to the system.

Conclusions

Although this has been, of necessity, a brief description of almost three years' experience with public access at the University of Guelph, we have reached many conclusions about the potential for this service, and the implications for library operations in the next decade.

Library users, particularly students, adapt very quickly to a computer terminal system and are able to cope successfully with quite sophisticated user functions. In 1979 a group of fourth-year computer science students at the university did an analysis of the circulation and catalog inquiry system for the library, and concluded that we needed, in addition to more terminals, the title display increased from three to five per screen, and title keyword search strategies combined with subject as a basic key.[1] (The latter we plan to do after the present catalog system is completely converted to the on-line mode.)

We also anticipate little need for any increase in our orientation program, even with the increased sophistication of functions available. The computer-assisted instruction which the sequential menus obviously supply seems to be the best orientation we could provide. Incidentally, the instructions on the remote-access module are presently very detailed for the novice user. We may be able to eliminate these in a few years.

Catalog Access—Card, COM or On-line

In the current controversy over catalog format, the University of Guelph Library has no doubt at all that, for a variety of reasons, there is only one way to go: on-line. We have had complete COM/fiche catalogs dispersed throughout the library as a supplement to the card catalog since 1973. Although they have been used and have some advantages, they cannot replace the card catalog in their currency. Support for this view comes from a recent study at the University of Oregon,[2] which concluded that most students simply will not use multiple files, and a library cannot afford to merge the files frequently enough to offset this problem, or to provide the immediate access of the card catalog.

The on-line catalog allows the user to relinquish dependence on the main-entry-centered card catalog, with its emphasis on standardization. If a minicomputer system (such as that described) allows integration in one access method of records of differing formats, then it is possible to provide the depth and method of bibliographic description required for each resource format. This is different for books, maps, serials, documents, and archives. Admittedly, the bibliographic utilities are enshrining the concept of standardized, in-depth record formats for all materials. In the long run, however, this is an expensive disservice to the local library user. Knowledge of other library holdings, now accessible from the union data base of the utilities, can be less expensively available through a distributed network.

The on-line catalog also bypasses AACR2 and all its related problems. An opportunity is now before North American libraries to rethink the purpose of the catalog, and to use automation to respond to user requirements.

Terminal Numbers and Type

In addition to commenting on menu and screen formats, the student group mentioned earlier also determined the number and distribution of public terminals which, based on observation of both card catalog and on-line inquiry use, they felt the library should have. The library staff estimated the need for an additional seven terminals (see table 1). These estimates indicate that the total number of library terminals required for a university of approximately 10,000 students is between twenty-three and thirty.

TABLE 1
NUMBER AND DISTRIBUTION OF PUBLIC TERMINALS

Location	Student Estimate	Library Estimate
Documentation center	2	3
Reserve room	2	3
Science division	4	4
Veterinary science division	2	2
Social science division	2	3
Humanities division	3	3
Card catalog (former) area	8	12
Total	23	30

The library is also considering dedicating at least two terminals to borrower file inquiry only. With this arrangement, students who merely want to know if they have books overdue do not need to be involved with students wanting catalog access.

The impact of the remote-access terminals, some of which will be located in the student residences, may well influence the decisions about numbers and locations of in-library terminals. Although many more terminals are already on order, a final decision will be made before May 1981, when we remove the card catalog.

Menu Drive v. Command Operations
   It has been suggested that it is more efficient in terms of internal computer operation to have a command-driven rather than a menu-driven system. While this may be true in theory, minicomputer technology makes the issue unimportant. Experience with a command-driven system eliminates it from consideration as a public tool. Cost of training sessions and procedural manuals for staff more than offset the slight benefits which might accrue from a "more efficient" operating system. Again, the quick response possible in on-line minicomputer technology allows the menu-driven system, with alternative options for new or experienced users, to operate without the necessity of library staff intervention or assistance.

On-line Access for All Systems
   The potentials of on-line public inquiry or access in an academic library are tremendous. As indicated earlier, different levels of bibliographic access, with different record formats for different materials, can all be accommodated; so can "on order" information from the acquisitions system, or periodical arrival information from the serial check-in system. Library or campus information, e.g., library hours, borrowing regulations, campus activities, or exam timetables, could form another data base that would be accessible on-line, making the library the focal point for all information on the campus—a position perhaps sought at present, but not necessarily achieved.

Summary
   In a recent article in the *Journal of Academic Librarianship*, Leonard suggested that: "we are not capitalizing upon computer technology's potential to enhance service to library users....Automation [in improving the efficiency of production of the manual card catalog] has been used to enhance technical productivity and not user access."[3] Experience with on-line public access and user inquiry at the University of Guelph Library demonstrates a different and desirable direction for the use of computers in libraries, one which abandons concentration on catalog formats and rules of entry, and adopts as its primary objective improved service to the library user.

REFERENCES

1. Benedict, Marylea, et al. "System Design Proposal." Guelph, Ontario, Dept. of Computer and Information Science, University of Guelph, 1979. (unpublished)

2. Dwyer, James R. "Public Response to an Academic Library Microcatalog," *Journal of Academic Librarianship* 5:132-41, July 1979.

3. Leonard, W. Patrick. "The Card Catalog Mentality, or We Have Always Done It This Way," *Journal of Academic Librarianship* 6:38, March 1980.

THOMAS T. HEWETT
Associate Professor of Psychology
Drexel University

CHARLES T. MEADOW
Professor of Information Science
Drexel University

A Study of the Measurement of User Performance

This paper reports on an attempt to measure the performance of users of interactive information retrieval systems.[1] The subjects studied were end users of the information who were doing their own interactive searches. The measures consist of a set of computerized diagnostic procedures applied to the sequences of commands used in querying the database. These diagnostics trigger various kinds of messages to the user. Presumably, the frequency with which a diagnostic is triggered is an index of the difficulties which the user may be having in doing a search. Although the utility to the user of the information retrieved is assumed to be the best overall measure of search outcome, it is the manner of using the system, not the search outcome, which is the focus of this report.

The studies described here were part of a larger project called Individualized Instruction for Data Access (IIDA). The goal of this project has been to provide a method for allowing direct user access to bibliographic searching. Thus, the attempt has been to develop a set of computer software packages which can provide on-line assistance to occasional users. This collection of programs is also intended to provide instruction, if needed, in the commands used in searching and search strategy. When originally conceived, the expected utility of IIDA lay in the area of what might be referred to as "problem-solving searches." These are searches where the end user of the information does not know exactly what the characteristics are of the desired set of references until they have actually been found. Consequently, it is very difficult for the user to describe the problem to an intermediary. There is no reason, however, why the IIDA user could not and should not make use of the system for all kinds of searches, if desired.

One intended IIDA user is a working scientist or engineer who may need access to the database only a few times a year, and consequently is not interested in training oriented toward those who become professional intermediaries. This person is assumed to be comfortable using computers, but not necessarily trained in their use. In addition, it is assumed that this user is a serious, well-intentioned searcher who is trying to use the system to solve a problem. The IIDA software and diagnostic procedures were created to help remove the barriers to access for these users. Minor modifications of the system, however, could make it available to a much wider audience.

DESCRIPTION OF IIDA

Physical Configuration

A schematic of the current physical arrangement of the IIDA system appears in figure 1. While it is now possible to package the IIDA software in a dedicated minicomputer, the experimental version of the IIDA software resided in a general-purpose, time-shared computer at the Massachusetts Institute of Technology. An IIDA user at a terminal communicates with the MIT computer which houses the IIDA software. This computer also houses the CONIT software, developed by Marcus and Reintjes, which performs some vital functions for the IIDA software.[2] When actively searching, the user is connected with DIALOG through either TELENET or TYMNET. The user employs the DIALOG language, and receives standard DIALOG responses. IIDA adds additional information and offers its own help facilities, but does not offer an alternative to using the DIALOG language. For the studies reported here, the database used was Compendex, but experimental work of various kinds has also made use of ERIC, NTIS and ONTAP ERIC. A detailed description of the IIDA software can be found in an IIDA report and in Toliver.[3]

User Introduction to IIDA

One of IIDA's design principles was to make its use as much like the direct use of DIALOG as possible, except when the user needs help. After logging on, the user is offered a brief, optional introduction to IIDA which, if accepted, provides a summary description of the system and of the available IIDA services. The user is also told how to ask for help and how to quit at any time.

While interacting with IIDA and the database, the user does so in either of two modes: instruction or assistance. In the assistance mode,

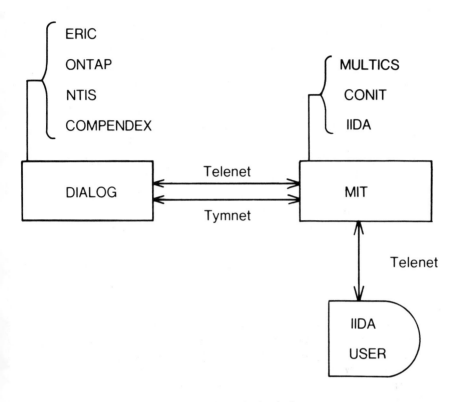

Figure 1. Schematic of IIDA physical arrangement

described later, the user begins searching, enters a series of DIALOG commands, and receives the same responses as he would without IIDA, if the commands are syntactically valid or do not trigger any of the diagnostic messages. If the user is not previously trained or desires a refresher course, he might begin with one of the computer-assisted training courses in the instruction mode.

Instruction Mode

The three exercises which constitute the instruction mode were designed to provide the user with: (1) the basic information necessary to do a search, (2) an opportunity to test these skills in a hands-on searching context, and (3) an opportunity to be exposed to advanced training in search commands and search strategy. While the user is allowed to begin use of IIDA at any point, and to proceed in any order, the recommended path for the novice is to do the three instructional exercises, in order, before going into the assistance mode.

"Canned" Search

In the first exercise, the user is introduced to the basic commands of DIALOG—BEGIN, SELECT, EXPAND, COMBINE, PAGE, TYPE, LOGOFF—through the medium of a "canned" search. The user is instructed to enter the commands which are given to him (i.e., he does not choose them; he is told, for example, to enter BEGIN 8). Then he sees a DIALOG response to the command, and the command is then explained. The intent is to maximize self-discovery. All of the commands are used in the context of an actual search, and so are used in the way they might be in a "real" search situation. In addition to this exposure to search commands and search strategy, the user is also introduced to the concept of a two-cycle search. A two-cycle search is, basically, one in which the user creates a set of references, and then, based on set size, browsing, or even intuition, cycles back to refine that set.

The user at this stage is also provided an introduction to the IIDA "help" facilities. These facilities enable a user to get: (1) the definitions of search commands, (2) advice on current problems, (3) information about commands given in the current search, (4) a list of the sets created up to the point at which help is requested, (5) a summary of the records viewed up to the point at which help is requested, (6) a list of the errors made, (7) a list of the descriptors used, and (8) instruction on how to change from the present exercise or mode to another. A more detailed description of this and the other instructional exercises can be found in an IIDA report.[4]

Practice Search

The second exercise is a practice search in which the novice user is asked to try out the use of some of the things learned in the first exercise. The user is also introduced to goal setting in searching, in that he is asked to set a search goal for a specific number of citations. There is no stipulation that he actually meet this goal, but several of the diagnostic messages that he might receive refer to it.

During exercise one, the computer is not connected to DIALOG, and the search which is done always produces the same results, since the information is stored in IIDA. During exercise two, the IIDA computer is linked with DIALOG, and the search performed is completely under the control of the user. Normally, it is expected that only the commands to which the user has been introduced will be encountered in this exercise, but there is no restriction on usable DIALOG commands. Similarly, IIDA suggests to the user some sample topics for searching in this exercise, but the user is free to search any desired topic. Those topics suggested to the user are generally simple ones for which there is a relatively high probability that the user will be able to do a successful search. An early success is desired to provide the satisfaction of seeing the system work correctly and productively.

Reference Walk

The third exercise in the instruction mode consists of a required look at summary descriptions of the available advanced instructional materials with the option for self-directed advanced training. These options are illustrated in figures 2 and 3. The contexts of this exercise include: (1) a review of the basic commands, (2) information about advanced commands, (3) an introduction to text searching, (4) further information about search strategy, (5) database description(s), (6) information about beginning and ending, and (7) a discussion of the IIDA facilities. As illustrated in figure 2, the user is introduced at a general level to topics on which considerably more detailed information is also available. Once this introduction is completed, users have a choice: they can either go on to the assistance mode, or return to do self-selected advanced training in various portions of exercise three (see fig. 3).

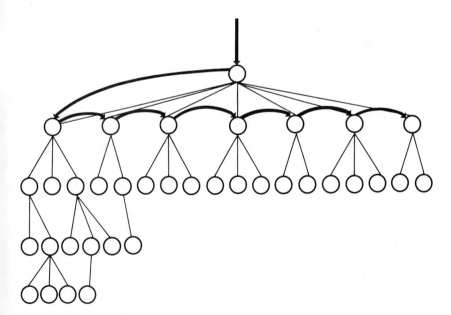

Figure 2. Reference walk in exercise three

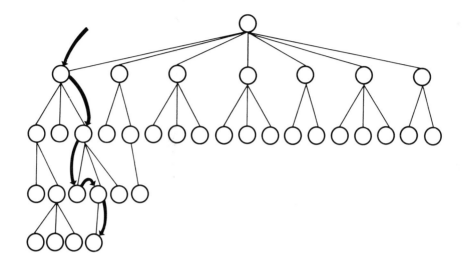

Figure 3. Self-selected advanced training in exercise three

Assistance Mode

In the assistance mode, the searcher performs his own search. The purpose of IIDA in the assistance mode is to offer assistance, to enable the user to do a search in DIALOG with a minimum of difficulty and interruption. Besides actually doing a search in the assistance mode, the user can, at any time, leave the search and enter any of the instructional exercises, or start the search over. Although it has not in fact been tested, in principle the user should be able, if patient enough, to do a search by going directly to the assistance mode without first using the three exercises in the instruction mode.

The three major features of the assistance mode, in addition to the flexibility it offers the user, are: (1) the reference help library, (2) quick advice, and (3) the set of diagnostics which monitor searcher behavior. As shown in figure 4, the reference help library contains all the information of exercise three in the instruction mode, but here the user is allowed free access to any information in the library at any level of detail selected. In addition, IIDA will also provide quick advice. Quick advice involves suggestions to the user on how to proceed in problem situations. In some cases, the nature of the problem is unambiguous, and IIDA can reference a particular bit of information in the help library. In other cases, the suggestion may simply be to use the help library. Once the desired information has been obtained, the user can signal for an automatic return to the search.

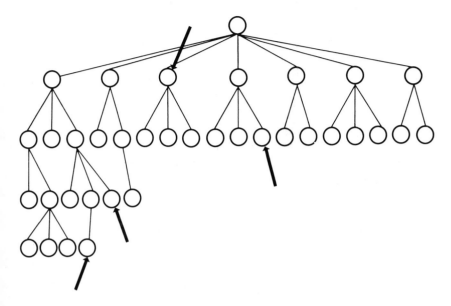

Figure 4. Free access to the reference help library during assisted searching

The most important aspect of the assistance mode, however, is the set of diagnostics which monitor searcher behavior and offer advice to the user. These diagnostics consist of a set of rules, clustered into categories, which are used by the computer to decide which messages to send to the user. Thus, IIDA is primarily a reactive system—the diagnostics are used to detect errors or tendencies which may lead to problems. If a diagnostic routine detects a problem, IIDA intrudes on the user with a statement of what the problem appears to be, and an indication of how to get advice or reference information.

DIAGNOSTIC PROCEDURES

Once a search begins, the user enters a series of DIALOG commands and receives the same responses as he would without IIDA, if the commands are syntactically valid. However, each command and its DIALOG response are intercepted by IIDA, parsed, and the components analyzed by the diagnostic procedures. If errors are discovered, IIDA intrudes into the communication between the user and DIALOG. In the case of a straightforward syntax error, the command is rejected (as it would be by DIALOG), and a specific statement of the problem is given the user.

The term *error* is used guardedly for other diagnostic procedures, since the nature of the problem is not one susceptible to algorithmic solution. Except for syntax errors, it is not possible to be entirely certain that a given command is "wrong." This judgment requires a knowledge of the goal and intentions of the user within a completely closed or bounded problem in which it is possible to specify all actions as either "right" or "wrong" on the basis of a set of well-defined rules. In this case, "wrong" and "error" are relative, since the diagnostics operate on the basis of certain heuristic principles. Thus, the diagnostic routines are intended to identify various behavior patterns which might lead to, or already be, a problem. The diagnostic messages are generally words of advice or caution to a user. They identify a problem or potential problem, and offer the user access to advice or instruction specific to that problem. The user is completely free to assume he knows what is going on, and to continue doing whatever triggered the diagnostic message. Given the open and unbounded nature of the problem involved, it may well be that the more experienced user knows exactly what he is doing.

Design Principles

The IIDA diagnostic system was based on the following principles:

1. The diagnostics have no access to any information about a search other than the search history; that is, IIDA can have no prior knowledge of how a given search "should" be performed.
2. Hence, IIDA is *reactive*; it helps a user decide how to proceed, given his performance to a point. It does not initiate directions in the sense of telling the user how to proceed with the search.
3. Diagnostics analyze user commands and the search service's response to them, determine problems, and point generally toward solutions. Emphasis is on encouraging self-discovery of solutions, e.g., when an error is detected, IIDA will suggest where advice or instruction is available, but will not force it on the user.
4. In making up the messages to be sent to the user, there was a conflict between the desire to offer the fullest explanation of any error (or apparent error) and the desire to avoid distracting the user by too much verbiage. The choice made was that all messages to the user reporting on error conditions should be as short as possible. Further, they should be unemotional. It is particularly important to avoid a conversational tone which users might interpret as pejorative ("You are wrong"), patronizing ("Good for you"), or cute ("Well, [name of user], you seem to have done this before"). This decision arose both from the designers' experiences with other systems which became abrasive quickly, and from the

belief that serious users will be content with straight information and will derive satisfaction from task accomplishment with a minimum of "chatter."

5. Certain errors must be brought to the user's attention each time they occur. For example, a syntactic error in formulating a command must be corrected if the command is to be executed. Other types of errors need be brought to the user's attention only if repeated often. This leads to the need for *thresholds, suppression* and *enhancement*.

For some errors, a *threshold* may be established allowing the error to be repeated a certain number of times before it is brought to the user's attention. In this case, the error message is *suppressed* until the threshold is reached. Once the threshold is reached, the message is sent, the index is reset, and when the new value is exceeded, a stronger or *enhanced* message may be sent to the user.

6. IIDA diagnostics do not, except indirectly, assist in the selection of appropriate search terms. Use of DIALOG's dictionary is stressed in the instructional material. Failure to use the EXPAND command (which searches the dictionary) may result in a diagnostic message, but IIDA does not suggest what actual terms to use.

7. Throughout the design of IIDA diagnostics, the intent was to focus the user's attention on the concept that a search is a structure to be designed and executed as a whole. At the same time, the user's easy access to help should relieve anxiety about mechanical detail by assuring him that forgotten details can easily be retrieved.

IIDA Concept of a Search

Conventionally, a DIALOG search starts with a BEGIN command and progresses through EXPANDs and SELECTs to one or more COMBINEs, and then to TYPE or DISPLAY.[5] After browsing, a user typically goes back through one or more of the commands—EXPAND, SELECT, COMBINE—and then browses again. Each excursion through EXPAND, SELECT, COMBINE, and TYPE, even if not all of these commands are used, constitutes a *cycle*. A sequence of commands of the same type constitutes a *string*. A cycle, then, consists of one or more strings, each of which consists of one or more commands of a given type. This is illustrated in figure 5, where strings of length one, two and three are shown, and these form two cycles. The second cycle begins when, following a TYPE command, the user reverts to SELECT. A number of the IIDA diagnostic procedures make use of this concept of strings and cycles.

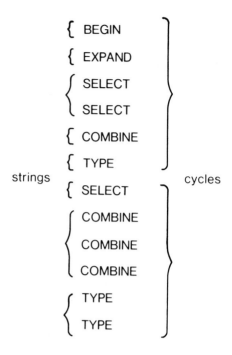

Figure 5. Strings and cycles in a search

Classes of Terms

The diagnostic procedures fall into the following three broad classes:

1. *Syntactic.* A DIALOG command may be viewed either as a simple sentence consisting of a verb and (usually) a noun phrase, or as a compound word. It is conventional computer science terminology to refer to the governing structural rules as *syntax*, although *morphology* may be more accurate, since a command lies somewhere between a compound word and a sentence. At any rate, the first class of diagnostics is concerned with the validity of a command, and this consideration is entirely context-free. The guiding operational rule is that a command is valid if and only if it would be accepted by DIALOG.

2. *Individual command usage.* Given a command that satisfies context-free structural rules, there may yet be problems that range from fatal errors (such as the use of an undefined set number in a COMBINE command) to mere inelegance of usage (such as repeating a previous command). The context of the analysis is limited. The diagnostics in this class consider the most recent command in the context of the

accumulated history of previous commands. In a sense, this form of analysis is syntactic in that it is more or less analogous to analysis of sentence structure in natural language.

3. *Command string usage.* Command string diagnostics are concerned with a set of commands as an entity, rather than with individual commands. These diagnostics are, in effect, concerned more with style than with mechanical exactitude.

Diagnostic Subclasses

In addition to performing diagnostic functions, the syntactic diagnostics are also an inseparable part of the IIDA command and response parsers, which maintain the history of the search and interact with communications control software. The nonsyntactic diagnostic procedures are, however, implemented as a series of rules, not unlike rules in a formal decision table.[6] Below, the diagnostics are described in terms of subclasses of diagnostics which represent groups of rules. The actual statement of the rules is very much dependent upon the specific database and search service used, while these subclasses remain fairly general.

1. *Syntactic.* All syntactic diagnostics begin with a left-to-right scan of the command text. If an unacceptable element is detected, the user is informed of what part of the command text is acceptable and at what point it becomes unacceptable. A response is made to all syntax errors.

2. *Individual commands.* These diagnostics consider a single command in the context of previous search history.

   a. *Repeated commands.* In DIALOG searching, in general, repeating a command with its argument is wasted motion. There are exceptions to this, such as if the searcher is working at a CRT terminal and does not have a printed record of his previous work, or if he wishes to use the PAGE or DISPLAY SETS commands. But to repeat a SELECT, COMBINE or TYPE generally is an indication of careless work. Further, IIDA can recognize what we call *essential repetition*, which is a repetition of the logical essence of a command without it being exactly the same command (e.g., COMBINE 1 * 2 is logically equivalent to COMBINE 2 * 1). A single instance of a command repetition fault is not serious.

   b. *Null sets.* Generally, a null set resulting from a SELECT command is an indication of poor choice of terms. If it results from a COMBINE command, it may represent no more than an infelicitous choice of Boolean expression. Null sets created with the SELECT command indicate that the user should take some steps, probably thesaurus browsing, to find better terms. Nulls created with the COMBINE command simply indicate the need for a different choice of expression. Repeated null set errors are assumed to be serious, and positive steps should be taken when they occur.

c. *Unused sets.* Sets are "used" when they are referred to in commands such as COMBINE or TYPE. If sets in any appreciable numbers are being created but never used in later commands, the assumption is that they are perhaps ill considered. This may be an indication of thrashing, i.e., the rapid change of direction of searching. IIDA counts the number of unused sets created in each cycle, but comments to the user only when, after a cycle, the number of unused sets is greater than it was at the end of the previous cycle, indicating a possible trend toward creating an increasing number of sets never used. Null sets are not charged to the unused set count. This is considered to be a moderately serious problem.

d. *Print format.* There are two types of print control errors. The first is use of a format that is likely to be uninformative. The extreme case here is a DIALOG format which gives accession numbers only, and is of no help to a searcher for browsing purposes. This is an example of a problem which might not occur often, but could unnerve a user when it does happen.

e. *Excessive printing.* The second type of print control error involves excessive printing. Novice users often print excessive numbers of records on-line because they are not used to sampling. They do not know the use of the off-line print commands, and they may be unaware of the costs. In addition, the experimental IIDA system terminals operated at 300 baud. At this speed, economy of time was important because of the limited number of hours during the day when the research studies could be conducted. Consequently, it was necessary to limit the number of citations a user could print with a single command. This limit varied with the format used.

f. *Response time.* The time between a machine's message and the input of the next command by the user is measured. Excessive consumption of time is, of course, expensive, and is also an indication of searcher difficulty. In addition to its pedagogical value, the time measurement can be used to terminate a user's session if the delay is extreme, indicating that the person has probably left the terminal but has not logged off. Time is not critical to search logic, but long delays inhibit the extent to which a person can remember all he has done previously. Time, in early experimental work, has been found a good discriminator between experienced and inexperienced searchers.[7]

3. *String diagnostics.* These are the diagnostics that look at sequences of commands.

a. *String and cycle length.* Tests are made for length of a string, by type of string, and for length of a cycle. The basic assumption is that any unusually long segment of a search might be an indication of a user problem.

b. *Thrashing.* This is changing the "direction" of a search rapidly or often, without pursuing any given direction far enough to see if it can work out. Searcher motivation for thrashing might be overly easy discouragement with preliminary results, such as getting a null set or an extremely large set from one search formulation; rather than trying to modify that formulation, the user turns to a completely different approach. At its worst, thrashing is indicative of random, uncontrolled behavior. It is, of course, not possible to measure "direction" precisely. It is done in somewhat arbitrary fashion by taking a measure of the similarity of the Boolean expressions in successive COMBINE commands. One consequence of this is that thrashing can occur only within a string of COMBINEs. The measure, called the *similarity index,* is made up from the percentage of implied terms common to the two expressions. "Implied" here means that an expression is expanded by replacing set numbers with their defining terms, and then the similarity count is done on terms, not set numbers. IIDA computes the number of terms in common, divides that first by the number of terms in one expression, then by the number in the other, and then takes the mean. This gives the similarity index between any two COMBINE commands. Thrashing is a mildly serious problem. A little bit of it does no particular harm. A great deal of it indicates a searcher is in trouble.

c. *Dwelling.* This is behavior opposite to thrashing. It is remaining with a search concept when it may be time to give up and try another approach. As with thrashing, dwelling is defined only within a string of COMBINEs. The similarity index is used to recognize dwelling, but this time it is in cases of similar COMBINE expressions, rather than dissimilar, that an IIDA message is sent to the user. Also used is the concept of convergence or divergence. The searcher will have been asked at the beginning of an IIDA-mediated search to state the search goal as a numeric step function. If a string of similar COMBINEs shows progress toward that goal, there is less concern about dwelling; if there is progress away from the goal, but the user remains with the same basic search concepts as indicated by the similarity index, he is dwelling. Regardless of convergence or divergence, if a similar string is too long, the user is dwelling. Dwelling can be a serious fault in that it might indicate a lack of understanding on the part of the searcher as to what a mechanical search, performed by someone of his skill level, is capable of producing. Perhaps the best example is a case in which the database simply does not have much information on the subject sought. Excessive dwelling does not help much; the problem is to realize the meagerness of the lode. d. *Relevance.* Much has been written about the nature of relevance, all of which is sidestepped in IIDA. Relevance in this context is a judgment made by a searcher about the value of search results to him. There is no way to control how he thinks about the concept, and there is no diversionary teaching on the subject. IIDA does ask the searcher to make a relevance judgment after each printing of a record (using the command TYPE or DISPLAY), unless the display was done using format 1 (which shows only accession number). The judgment is made on a five-point scale, from irrelevant to highly relevant, with "1" representing "irrelevant." Diagnostics are performed on the average relevance figures for a group of records displayed with a single command, as long as at least three records are typed. Relevance diagnostics are not based upon faults or search errors, but they are used to direct the searcher's attention to the fact that a particular set seems not to be fruitful, or that a previously examined set yielded higher relevance scores. Although low average relevance figures give no hint as to the remedy, the problem detected is a serious one—the searcher has come to the end of a cycle and is dissatisfied with the results according to his own definition of relevance. If this condition recurs repeatedly at the end of cycles, the entire approach to the search comes into question.

TESTING

The testing of the diagnostics as a way of assessing user performance necessarily involves the testing of users as well. There have been essentially three major phases of this testing. These consisted of the pilot testing of the entire system to ensure that it functioned as intended, a baseline or benchmark study conducted to establish a set of reference points for the operation of the diagnostics, and a training method study done to determine whether the diagnostics operate differently with people trained in differing ways.

Pilot Testing

The pilot testing conducted with IIDA was oriented primarily toward the discovery of either programming or conceptual problems with the operation of the system. Among the groups working with the system during this early testing were undergraduate computer science majors who acted as users and who were challenged to find the problems. In addition, a number of faculty and graduate students from Drexel's School of Library and Information Science were invited to review the operation of the system and give their advice and comments. All of the members of this latter group were trained searchers, and some of them are regularly involved in the training of searchers. Another pilot test group consisted of a number of undergraduate engineering majors, who did the search training as part of a course on technical writing. The experiences and feedback of each of these user groups resulted in successive changes and refinements in the operation of the system. For example, extensive cross-comparison of the search transcripts from the technical writing students and the records kept by IIDA provided a check which ensured that the machine record-keeping programs did what they were programmed to do.

This kind of pilot testing is an indispensable part of the development of any system as large and complex, and as user-oriented, as IIDA. Because of their closeness to the system and the problems of conceptual design, the system designers are at times not the best judges of what material should be viewed by, or must be explained to, the user. The following examples, which were easily corrected by revision of user instructions or of the instructional material, illustrate this point well. Even though their initial classroom description of IIDA was of a computer system that would assist them in retrieving references for use in writing required course papers, a few of the technical writing students started the training initially expecting to retrieve facts about their search topic rather than references relevant to the topic. Other students did not seem to realize that the commands encountered in exercise one should be learned for future use. Another problem which showed up in the early stages of training the technical writing students involved the effects of search commands in the context of a search. The version of exercise one used with these students illustrated a search on the topic of library automation. At one point in this search, the user was told to EXPAND LIBRARY. A few of the users subsequently thought that the next time they wanted to EXPAND a term, they were to enter EXPAND LIBRARY, no matter what term was to be expanded.[8]

Baseline Study

The baseline study was conducted in 1979 at the Exxon Research and Egnineering Company facility at Florham Park, New Jersey.[9] The study design called for collecting data on the searches performed by twenty-five searchers who were trained and assisted by IIDA. In addition, twenty-five comparable searches were to be done by the information retrieval staff on site. The intent here was to use the intermediated searches to provide a profile of diagnostic usage for comparison with the diagnostics usage of the IIDA users. It was anticipated that significant differences between the two groups of searches would reveal deficiencies in the IIDA training and assistance, which would then be subsequently corrected by appropriate modifications of the system.

Procedure

Participants in this study consisted of fifty Exxon research engineers employed at the Florham Park site who had been recruited by mail. Approximately 2200 letters were sent out offering the opportunity for technical personnel to do on-line searching on their own via the IIDA system. Approximately 150 responses were received. The names were randomized so that date of response, level of position within the company, and the department and section would not be considerations for participation in the study. From this randomized list, twenty-five participants were then randomly assigned to the IIDA training group, and twenty-five were randomly assigned to the intermediated group.

Participants assigned to the IIDA training group were scheduled for two sessions which involved the IIDA training followed by two IIDA-assisted searches on topics of their own choosing. Each of these participants filled out a post-search questionnaire after completing the second search. Participants assigned to the intermediated group brought their next search topic to one of the Information Center staff, as they would normally do. This search, however, was done by the intermediary through IIDA with all IIDA responses and messages suppressed. Thus, the only aspects of IIDA working for the intermediated searches were the record-keeping functions, which kept track of the search history and of the number of times various diagnostic rules were triggered by the searching behavior of the intermediary. A post-search questionnaire was given to each of the participants in the intermediated group, along with the results of the search requested. Since they had been recruited with an offer of search training, these participants were scheduled for IIDA search training after completing the post-search questionnaire.

Results

The post-search questionnaire for participants in both the IIDA and the intermediated groups included a question which asked what percentage of the references retrieved were: (1) very useful, (2) useful, (3) useless. For purposes of analysis, the "very useful" and "useful" categories were combined into the single category, "useful." The difference between the two groups on this measure was not significant (Mann-Whitney U Test, $p > 0.05$), with the IIDA-trained group reporting an average of 52.5 percent useful references, and the intermediated group an average of 49.3 percent useful references retrieved. Consequently, it appears that the results of the searches were valued equally by those who did their own searches and those who had a search done for them.

Turning to the diagnostics, the pattern is one in which there appear to be no differences between the two sets of searches. The mean frequencies for each group of searches for each of the three major categories of diagnostics—syntax, the individual command usage or "local" diagnostics, and the command string usage or "global" diagnostics—are illustrated in figure 6. For each of these classes of diagnostics, the differences betwen the two sets of searches were not statistically significant (Mann-Whitney U Test, p > 0.05). This finding also holds true for each of the subcategories of diagnostics contained within each major category.

In light of the intent of this study, i.e., to provide a set of diagnostic bench-mark criteria against which to assess the performance of the IIDA-trained and assisted searchers, it was surprising to discover a lack of significant differences between the two groups of searches. A significant difference on one or more of the diagnostics would have pointed toward some deficiency in the IIDA training, or in the usefulness of the diagnostic messages during IIDA-assisted searching. This would have led to revision of one or both aspects of the system. The finding of no significant differences poses a potential problem in that this could suggest either that the IIDA training and IIDA diagnostics work well, or that they are totally irrelevant. One reason for arguing that the training and diagnostic assistance worked as intended is that the end user evaluation of the utility of the information retrieved in the searches did not differ significantly between the two groups. This means that a group of individuals who had never before done on-line searching were able, with IIDA training and assistance, to do searches which produced results containing as much useful information as contained in searches done by professional searchers. Under these circumstances, the notion that the diagnostics are irrelevant as measures of searcher performance seems implausible.

It should be mentioned in passing that there is one subcategory of diagnostic information which is not included in the results reported in figure 6. Since the intermediaries did their searches with IIDA suppressed, they were not asked by the system to make relevance judgments on the references typed out. Consequently, this diagnostic category was not included in the data of the IIDA users when comparisons were conducted between the IIDA-assisted and the intermediated searches.

Training Method Study

The second major test of IIDA and the diagnostics took place at the Exxon Research and Engineering Company facility in Linden, New Jersey, during the winter months of 1979-80. This study involved a comparison of the searches done by IIDA-trained and assisted searchers with those

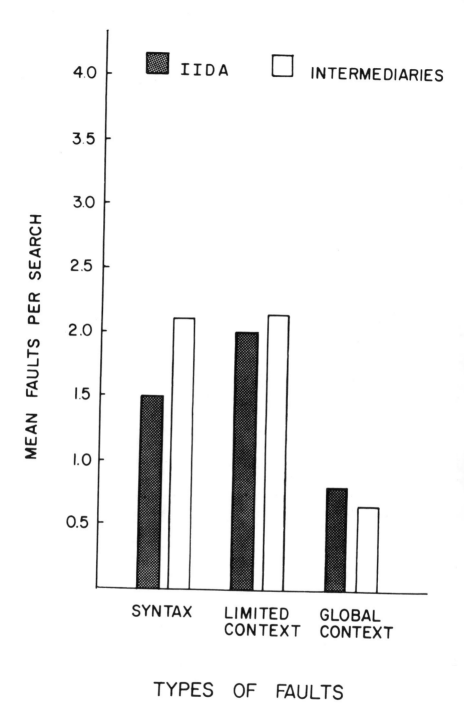

Figure 6. Average frequencies for three major classes of faults of Florham Park

done by a group of searchers who were also assisted by IIDA, but who had been trained in a half-day classroom training session. The intent of this study was to test the instructional procedures and materials involved in IIDA training against a more frequently used and conventional training method. Presumably a human instructor is more responsive to the problems which a student may encounter, and presumably the student has a greater range of questions which can be asked of a human instructor, especially since IIDA is not designed to be a question-answering system. Consequently, it was anticipated that significant differences between the two groups of searchers would reveal deficiencies in the IIDA training, which would subsequently be corrected by appropriate modifications of the system.[10]

Procedure

Participants in this study were primarily research chemists and other scientists. Participants were again recruited by mail, with letters sent to the entire research staff describing the opportunity for bibliographic search training and asking for volunteers. As with the earlier study, about 150 responses were received. From the list of volunteers, fifty were randomly selected to participate. Twenty-five volunteers were randomly assigned to receive IIDA training and then do two IIDA-assisted searches, while the other twenty-five were assigned to the conventional training sessions, with two IIDA-assisted searches following training. All participants in the conventionally trained group received training by Exxon Information Center staff in one of four morning sessions. All of the training sessions used the same training materials (handouts, etc.), covered the same material, and allowed some on-line time for the users to practice what they had learned.

Results

In this study, the post-search questionnaire, which was administered after completion of the second IIDA-assisted search, asked the user to decide what percentage of the references retrieved had been: (1) very useful, (2) useful, (3) useless. Again, the first two categories were combined into the single category, "useful." The difference between the two groups, while apparently large, was not significant (Mann-Whitney U Test, $p > 0.05$), with the IIDA-trained group reporting an average of 46.6 percent and the conventionally trained group an average of 62.9 percent useful references retrieved.

Concerning the diagnostics, again there appear to be no differences between the two sets of searches. The mean frequencies for each group of searches for each of the three major categories of diagnostics are illustrated in figure 7. It should be noted that the data in this study do include the subcategory of relevance diagnostics in the "global" diagnostics, since both groups did their search with IIDA fully operational rather than suppressed (as was the case for the intermediated searches done in the study described earlier). For each of the three categories of diagnostics, the differences between the two sets of searches are not statistically significant (Mann-Whitney U Test, $p > 0.05$). Furthermore, individual comparison of the subcategories of diagnostics indicated no significant differences between the two groups.

Considering that the purpose of the study was to compare IIDA training with a more conventional method, the lack of significant differences between the two groups was surprising. A significant difference on one or more diagnostic measures would have indicated either a flaw in the IIDA training materials or in the diagnostic messages during assisted searching. The result would be a revamping of one or both parts of the system. Since no significant differences were discovered, there is the problem of interpreting the results, except for the fact that the groups were able to retrieve a significant percentage of useful references during their searches. Presumably this represents something which neither group would have been able to accomplish if simply turned loose with a terminal without any training. Further, the two groups did not differ in their estimates of the percentage of useful references retrieved. This pattern of results argues strongly that IIDA training, as it is presently structured, represents a viable alternative to the type of conventional training with which it was compared.

Looking at the data from both studies and comparing both sites by diagnostic category, there were no significant differences in the usage of the diagnostics frome one site to the other. In addition, judgments made by users about the percentage of useful references retrieved did not differ significantly from one site to the other. Thus, the two groups trained at Linden did not produce results appreciably different from those obtained for the group of intermediated searches done at Florham Park. It should also be mentioned that the variability in the measures, including percentage of useful references retrieved, did not differ significantly from one group to another. One final point to be noted is that the users seemed to like IIDA. Approximately 90 percent of the users, either trained and assisted by IIDA or just assisted by IIDA, said they would recommend use of IIDA to their friends.

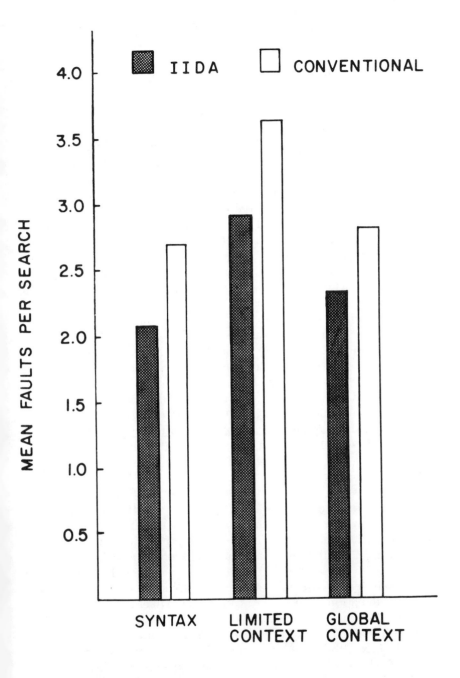

Figure 7. Average frequencies for three major classes of faults at Linden

DISCUSSION AND CONCLUSIONS

User Performance

It is not possible to separate completely the performance of the IIDA diagnostics from the performance of the IIDA users. Focusing first on the users, however, the data suggest that IIDA users did searches which were, on two kinds of measures, done as well as those done by a professional searcher. First, in the ratings of the utility of the overall results of the searches, there was no significant difference between the results obtained by the professional searcher and those obtained by the user performing his own search. Second, no significant differences were found in the number of IIDA-detected errors or faults between the newly trained, IIDA-assisted searchers and the professional searchers. Together, these findings imply that the results of the searching were about equal, and that the performance of the searchers was about equal.

It was initially a surprise to find that the error/fault rate seemed about equal between the professional and neophyte searchers. IIDA was designed to produce acceptable results for its users, but it was never expected that the step-by-step performance would match that of professionals. There are, however, some mitigating circumstances which may have handicapped the professionals somewhat. For example, the Exxon professional searchers are used to working with 1200-baud terminals. With these terminals, more on-line typing is acceptable than with the 300-baud terminals used for IIDA searching. Hence, the professional staff was accustomed to doing a great deal of on-line printing, often exceeding the limit allowed for IIDA users working with the slower terminal. Also, IIDA's design was fixed just before Lockheed announced the new SUPER SELECT command.[II] Thus, this command was not included in the IIDA training materials, and its syntax was not recognized by IIDA's parser.

Although the intermediaries knew about these limitations, an inadvertent transfer of habits from the usual search context into the IIDA search context could have introduced some faults or errors which might not otherwise have occurred. For example, if a searcher used SUPER SELECT for set combination, then there was an increased likelihood of the appearance of a large number of SELECT commands without any COMBINE command. This could then trigger an "excessive string length" diagnostic. Consequently, although it is not possible to assign numerical values, there is reason to believe that the professional searchers might have had a higher error/fault rate than normal. However, it is certainly the case that the IIDA searchers performed respectably well, and, in terms of final outcome, the users who did their own searching using IIDA achieved results equivalent in utility to those who worked through intermediaries.

The other surprise in the results on user performance came in the findings that the two different user groups trained by different methods did not differ appreciably either on the diagnostic measures or in the percentage of useful references retrieved. The original design specifications for IIDA did not envision a system which would be competitive with more conventional training approaches. Rather, the intent was to provide an avenue of access for individuals who could not or would not take a conventional training course, but who still wanted personal (rather than intermediated) access to a database. It had been assumed that comparisons between the two different training methods would highlight difficulties with IIDA. One reasonable guess as to the reason for the pattern of results reported here is that, while the human instructor may well have been more flexible and responsive in assisting the student and in answering questions, the design of IIDA does, as intended, enable the user to discover where to go to get the information needed to answer questions.

Performance of the Diagnostics

Earlier, the possibility was mentioned that the IIDA diagnostics, rather than indexing various aspects of searcher behavior, might be irrelevant to the process of searching. This would account for the lack of significant differences between IIDA users and professionals, and between IIDA-trained and conventionally trained users, on these measures. This explanation seems, however, to be less reasonable than the idea that the system is working as it was designed to work. One reason for not assuming that the diagnostics are irrelevant as indices of searching behavior is that the diagnostics were all empirically developed. In other words, they were all designed to index and deal with problems encountered by searchers which have been observed by the designers and/or reported in the literature by others.

Furthermore, the relative frequencies of the various types of errors or faults correspond reasonably well with the intuitions which originally led to the development of the diagnostics. Figure 8 shows the mean number of occurrences per search of the various subcategories of diagnostics, aggregated over the entire study. Also indicated are the 95 percent confidence limits for each type of diagnostic. The diagnostics which were triggered most commonly were syntax, relevance and null set generation. A second group consists of string length faults and excessive printing. The third group, of six fault types, is characterized by relatively low frequency of occurrence; in fact, some of the confidence intervals include zero. These last six are: response time, command repetition, print format, unused sets, dwelling, and thrashing. Even though these diagnostics were triggered relatively infrequently, they are probably worth keeping, since the response to the open-ended questions on the post-search questionnaire suggested that for an occasional user they were useful.

In general, the diagnostics are mutually independent in that the triggering of one has no implication as to whether the others will be triggered. There are, however, some exceptions where there is an interrelation. For example, a string length diagnostic is triggered whenever a certain number (n) of successive commands of any given type is received. A dwelling or thrashing diagnostic requires both a string of COMBINE commands and certain conditions with respect to the arguments of the COMBINEs. In other words, there must be a string of length m, plus other conditions. If the threshold on the string length diagnostic were set short enough, that is, if $n < m$, a user entering a string of COMBINEs would be warned against continuing that pursuit before the dwelling or thrashing rules and diagnostic messages could take effect. The various thresholds were set heuristically, and these settings have some effect on which rules a searcher is deemed to have violated. Hence, a slight change in the thresholds might have resulted in the occurrence of one type of diagnostic rather than the other.

Conclusions from the Diagnostics

Overall, it seems that the various categories of diagnostics do represent a reasonable set of measures of the performance of on-line searchers. The fact that the novice searchers studied were able to achieve a degree of satisfaction with the final results equal to that achieved through professional searchers suggest that, with the help of the IIDA diagnostics, these searchers performed the search as well as the professionals. Enabling them to do so was the goal of the IIDA assistance mode program.

This equivalence would imply that when a searcher has an error or fault rate widely divergent from those reported, there also exists a difference in performance in some area of searching behavior. In the case of excessive errors or faults, this is presumably self-correcting over time with repeated exposure to the diagnostic messages and practice. In the case of a low error rate, the deviation may indicate a person ready for a language of greater complexity. That is, sustained error-free performance probably means that the user is ready to take on a language capable of greater logical power. Such languages are typically more complex and demanding in terms of what the user must know.

One important caution is that the IIDA diagnostics were designed for use in a certain limited context, that of the training and assistance of the kind of users described in the introduction to this paper and in the user

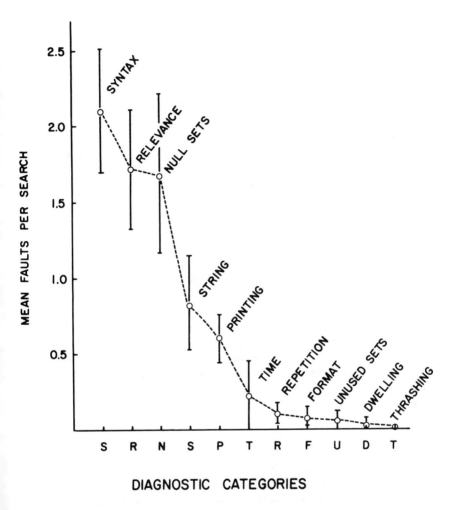

Figure 8. Average frequencies for the diagnostic categories for all users

studies conducted. There is some indication in the experiences of the professionals that when the diagnostics were employed with highly experienced searchers, they may not be the most appropriate procedures, i.e., there are times when the diagnostics may have been triggered by relatively sophisticated searcher behavior which is appropriate in one context, but not in situations with which IIDA was designed to cope.

Future Research

Inasmuch as the conclusions drawn about the effectiveness of the diagnostics are not as clear as might be desirable, several additional directions for future research should be followed:

1. *Diagnostic evaluation.* The overall requirements for evaluation of the project as a whole, as well as the available resources, dictated that some studies have a higher priority than others. This led to concentration on the evaluation of IIDA as a system rather than a more direct focus on the diagnostic component of the system. A future evaluation devoted solely to the question of the performance of the diagnostic system, with and without various kinds of training in advance, would be both useful and desirable.

2. *Longitudinal study.* A real limitation of studies such as those described here, and of many others on searcher behavior, is the relatively short amount of time between the participants' first exposure to the system and the evaluation of their performance or of the system performance. In addition, there seems to have been little or no testing of information system users at several points to investigate development or change over an extended period of time. In the studies described above, the volunteer subjects generally wanted to do the whole set of exercises, and then do their searching in a relatively short time. It seems particularly desirable that a long-range study be done, over a period of a year or so, focusing on how different people adapt to a new system, how quickly they adapt, how their behavior changes over time, and how it changes as the result of multiple search experiences.

3. *Adaptation to user skill level.* As noted above, it is not expected that the same diagnostics will be equally useful or desirable for all user skill levels. It would be desirable not only to test the diagnostics on persons of differing skill levels, but to test different variations of the diagnostics. In particular, it seems desirable to test whether, by varying the thresholds in the existing set of diagnostics as a function of actual prior performance, it is possible to get them to perform adequately with persons of different skill levels. That is, can they be made adaptive?

4. *Various user groups.* Although the original target user group for IIDA consisted of technically trained individuals interested in a particular class of search problems, there now seems to be no reason not to attempt extension of IIDA. The technically or scientifically trained users may be only one of several groups who would find IIDA attractive and useful. In particular, it seems desirable to determine whether or not a system such as IIDA can be used to provide direct database access for a wide variety of possible end users interested in a wide variety of search problems.

In summary, it seems that a new idea has been fairly tested in the very environment for which the concept was intended. Indeed, one of the important characteristics of the two studies discussed is that there appeared to be no differences among the results produced by the various user groups when there had been every reason to expect a number of differences. While some aspects of these results are not entirely conclusive, they support the idea that the IIDA diagnostic procedures did adequately measure important aspects of user performance. What is more certain, however, is that the IIDA system represents a way of training and assisting novice users to search databases with a level of performance that matches that of more experienced searchers. Furthermore, IIDA clearly represents a viable alternative to gaining direct database access for those end users who cannot or will not engage in more conventional forms of serach training.

REFERENCES

1. The work reported here was sponsored in part by the National Science Foundation, Division of Information Science and Technology, under Grant No. DSI 77-26524. The two user studies were also supported in part by a grant from Exxon Research and Engineering Company, which also made space available for the conduct of the studies. Special thanks are owed to Barbara Lawrence of Exxon, who played a major role in enabling the user studies to be set up, and to the staff members and the participant users of the Exxon information retrieval services at the sites where the studies were conducted. Finally, the authors thank Robert Rich, the IIDA consultant on evaluation, whose insightful comments were always valued even when not heeded.

2. Marcus, R.W., and Reintjes, F.J. "Experiments and Analysis on a Computer Interface to an Information Retrieval Network" (NSF Grant No. IST 76-82117). Cambridge, Mass., MIT Laboratory for Information and Decision Systems, 1979.

3. Individualized Instruction for Data Access (IIDA). Quarterly Report No. 6 (NSF Grant No. DSI 77-26524). Philadelphia, School of Library and Information Science, Drexel University, and Franklin Research Center, Sept. 1979; and Toliver, David E. "A Program for Machine-Mediated Searching," Information Processing & Management. (In press.)

4. Individualized Instruction for Data Access (IIDA). Quarterly Report No. 5 (NSF Grant No. DSI 77-26524). Philadelphia, School of Library and Information Science, Drexel University, and Franklin Research Center, June 1979.

5. A Guide to DIALOG Searching. Palo Alto, Calif., Lockheed DIALOG Information Retrieval Service, 1979.

6. For a full description of these rules, see: Individualized Instruction for Data Access (IIDA). Quarterly Report No. 4 (NSF Grant No. DSI 77-26524). Philadelphia, School of Library and Information Science, Drexel University, and Franklin Research Center, March 1979. (ED179 195)

7. Fenichel, Carol H. Online Information Retrieval: Identification of Measures that Discriminate among Users with Different Levels and Types of Experience. Philadelphia, School of Library and Information Science, Drexel University, 1979.

8. Individualized Instruction for Data Access (IIDA). Quarterly Report No. 7 (NSF Grant No. DSI 77-26524). Philadelphia, School of Library and Information Science, Drexel University, Dec. 1979.

9. Individualized Instruction for Data Access (IIDA). Quarterly Report No. 8 (NSF

Grant No. DSI 77-26524). Philadelphia, School of Library and Information Science, Drexel University, March 1980.

10. Ibid.

11. *Guide to DIALOG Searching*, op. cit., pp. 3-6.

MARK S. FOX
Research Scientist
The Robotics Institute
Carnegie-Mellon University

ANDREW J. PALAY
Research Assistant
Computer Science Department
Carnegie-Mellon University

Machine-Assisted Browsing
for the Naïve User

Introduction

The purpose of this paper is to demonstrate how a radically different approach to the storage and retrieval of information can result in: (1) a reduction in the need for user sophistication in the use of information systems, and (2) the support of a browsing approach to information system searching. Our approach promotes the view that information system databases should be structured for people, not machines. Many of the problems associated with information systems occur precisely at the interface between the user and information storage. The purpose of the interface is to map user requests onto the database structure. The more "machine-like" the interface, the faster the mapping. As interfaces become more sophisticated (i.e., allow the user to express requests in a more natural form such as natural language), more processing is required to carry out the mapping. And as processing time increases, certain types of search processes (e.g., browsing) become increasingly difficult to provide at a reasonable response rate. Until the time when processing power can meet the real-time needs of system users, information system design and construction should conform to user needs, meaning that the physical structure should be tailored to the user's view (logical structure) of the database, reducing mapping and search time.

In the following discussion, we will describe the BROWSE system, a database browsing system for computer-naïve users.[1] The primary application of the BROWSE system is to allow browsing access to the Carnegie-Mellon University Computer Science Department library collection, but it can be used for other applications, such as the automated dictionary.[2]

We will begin by characterizing our view of the naïve user. Browsing will then be defined, followed by a detailed example of browsing in the BROWSE system. This is followed by an evaluation of BROWSE as a browsing tool for the naïve user. Lastly, we describe the BROWSE system software used to generate browsable information systems.

Characterizing the Naïve User for System Design

A common misconception is that the naïve user of an information system has little or no computer-related experience. Such is not necessarily the case. Naïveté can take many forms:

Computer Naïveté: The person has no experience with a computer. "Intelligent" interaction with a machine is an alien concept. The individual may be reluctant or apprehensive about approaching information systems.

Interface Naïveté: Many information system interfaces are complex and idiosyncratic, requiring many hours of training. New users are unable to use such systems. Information specialists act as intermediaries. Research in natural language understanding is an attempt to make the interface more comfortable.[3]

Information Structure Naïveté: How information is structured in the database, i.e., *what* the categorization hierarchies, is often different from the user's view of the structure. Hence, the ability to specify an information request does not imply that anything will be found.

Category Naïveté: Given that the user does not possess any of the above naïvities, information access can still be hampered. How information is categorized can vary among categorizers. Even if the user knows the categorization hierarchy, the category a user thinks suitable for an entry may not be the one chosen by the categorizer.

Any of these can impede the successful acquisition of information. Hence, information systems must be designed to remove these impediments.

Ignoring computer naïveté, we propose three principles for the design of user-accessible information systems: (1) principle of interface perspicuity, (2) principle of structure perspicuity, and (3) principle of category perspicuity. These principles directly correspond to the last three naïveties listed above. They state that the interface, database structure, and categorization methods must be either apparent to the user or easily learned. Hence, any information system design must account for these principles if it is to be used by naïve users.

Just as important as defining these principles are the methodologies for measuring adherence to them. In measuring interface perspicuity, Card and others have identified several interface performance factors:

Time: How long does it take a user to accomplish a given set of tasks using the system?

Errors: How many errors does a user make and how serious are they?

Learning: How long does it take a naïve user to learn how to use the system in order to do a given set of tasks?

Functionality: What range of tasks can a user do with the system?

Recall: How easy it is for a user to recall how to use the system on a task that he has not done for some time?

Concentration: How many things does a user have to keep in mind while using the system?

Fatigue: How tired do users get when they use the system for extended periods?[4]

An interface should minimize time, errors, learning, and fatigue while maximizing functionality, recall and concentration. What these actual values should be depends on the application. Structure and categorization perspicuity can be measured by experiment: do users find the information they want? Bates has done such an analysis, showing that only 33 percent of library searchers who thought they were successful actually were.[5] How well BROWSE satisfies these factors is discussed later in the paper.

Search Methods: Browsing v. Parameterized Search

The majority of research in the area of database access has focused on the area of parameterized search (PS). PS can be characterized as strictly focused, in the sense that the user must specify exactly the set of attributes that the records must have, e.g., "Get me all the records for items written by Fox about learning." Besides the naïveté problems discussed above, PS systems do not allow quick and easy access to related records. In order to access related material, a new set of search parameters must be specified. Access to related information is the essence of browsing.

Browsing can be characterized as a heuristic search in a well-connected space of records. In particular, browsing can be viewed as an iterative, five-step process:

1. Choose a browsing attribute, such as a category, author, keyword, etc.
2. Access and peruse entries via the chosen attribute (e.g., books, technical reports, etc.).
3. Narrow perusal (search) to small subset.
4. Examine a small subset of entries to confirm interest and find new information.
5. If an entry suggests a new search attribute, then go to step 1 or else go to step 2.

Each of the browsing steps described above is important and is just barely supported in a library. That is, only the author and category attributes are indexed, and distances between shelves impede searches. Both libraries and information systems must provide the ability to search and examine. Even more important, many search attributes must be accessible and new attributes easily searched. Some of the search heuristics most commonly used in browsing library databases are:

1. If book x is interesting, then what else has the author of x written?
2. If book x is interesting, then what other books are in the same category?
3. If a symposium article is interesting, then what else appeared in the same symposium?
4. If the author of an interesting paper is from an institution x, then what else has been published at that institution?
5. If there is an interesting paper in a journal, then what else appeared in that journal?

The goal of the BROWSE system is to provide browsing access to databases by building the search heuristics directly into the database as quick-access paths between related records. This includes: (1) providing a simple man-machine interface that takes little training to master, (2) presenting the system in such a way that its logical structure is easily and quickly understood, and (3) providing a browsing-style approach to database searching.

An Example

A BROWSE system database consists of a set of frames. A frame is a single CRT (television) screen of information. The purpose of the frame is to provide information to the user, and to provide quick access to further, related information. Options provide links to related frames. A user moves between the frames by selecting an option, which results in the display of a new frame. Figure 1 is an example from a BROWSE database developed for an on-line library catalog system.

The first frame (fig. 1) welcomes the user to the BROWSE system. In the upper right-hand corner of every frame is the name of the frame (in this case, ZOG1). At the bottom of the frame is a set of standard options (*help, back, next,..., find*). These options, called global pads, will appear in every frame. They provide a set of system functions that are useful throughout the entire network. The first frame consists of the text welcoming the user to the BROWSE system and three options. The first option allows the user to continue receiving instruction on how to use the BROWSE system. The second option allows the user to move directly to the top of the classifica-

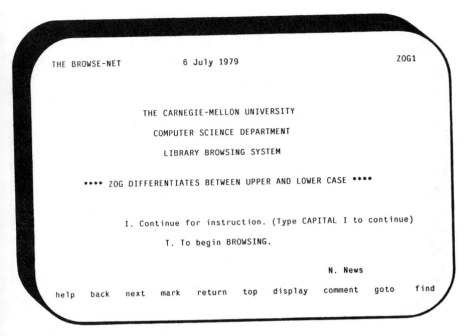

THE BROWSE-NET   6 July 1979   ZOG1

THE CARNEGIE-MELLON UNIVERSITY

COMPUTER SCIENCE DEPARTMENT

LIBRARY BROWSING SYSTEM

•••• ZOG DIFFERENTIATES BETWEEN UPPER AND LOWER CASE ••••

I. Continue for instruction. (Type CAPITAL I to continue)

T. To begin BROWSING.

N. News

help   back   next   mark   return   top   display   comment   goto   find

Figure 1

tion hierarchy. The third option allows the user to get news describing changes to the system. To select an option, the user types in the first letter of the option ("I" to select the first option, "T" for the second, "N" for the third). If there is a pointing device (mouse, touch screen, etc.) available, then the user need only point to the option in order to select it. The naïve user would continue by selecting the "I" option for more instruction. An experienced user would select option T, thus displaying the top of the classification hierarchy (fig. 2). There are twelve options to this frame. Options that contain a dash (—) after the first two characters do not point to any other frames. They are included as pointers to information which one day will be included. An important property of the BROWSE system is that it can support multiple views of the database. At present, only the Computing Review classification (1976) and a new entries list are available.

By selecting option 1, the user moves on to the top of the Computing Review classification hierarchy (fig. 3). The frames forming the classification hierarchy each contain a title (0: Computer Science), a definition section, a list of subcategories, an "entry list" option (E), a "lost map" option (L), and a "parameterized search" option (S). If there are additional

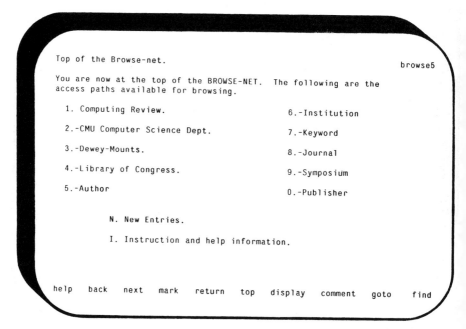

Figure 2

subcategories, then a "more selections" option is included (M). Finally, if there is a designated primary supracategory, then an option (P) is included that links the current classification frame to its primary supracategory. The entry list option points to a list of the entries that have been directly classified under the current category. In this case there are no such entries. Finally, the parameterized search option causes the system to begin a parameterized search and proceed to a set of frames that allows the user to specify the parameters.

The initial goal of this sample session is to browse through the database for information related to learning. By selecting the option for Applications, the user learns that the category includes cognitive processes (fig. 4). By selecting the "more selections" option (M), the user discovers that Artificial Intelligence is one of the subcategories of Applications (fig. 5). If Applications was not a useful category, the P option could be selected to go back up the hierarchy, to allow the user to select another search path.

By selecting option 2, the user moves to the frame describing Artificial Intelligence (fig. 6) and discovers that learning is one of the subcategories (Learning and Adaptive Systems). Note that an entry frame exists for this category. If the user wanted to see entries directly classified under Artificial

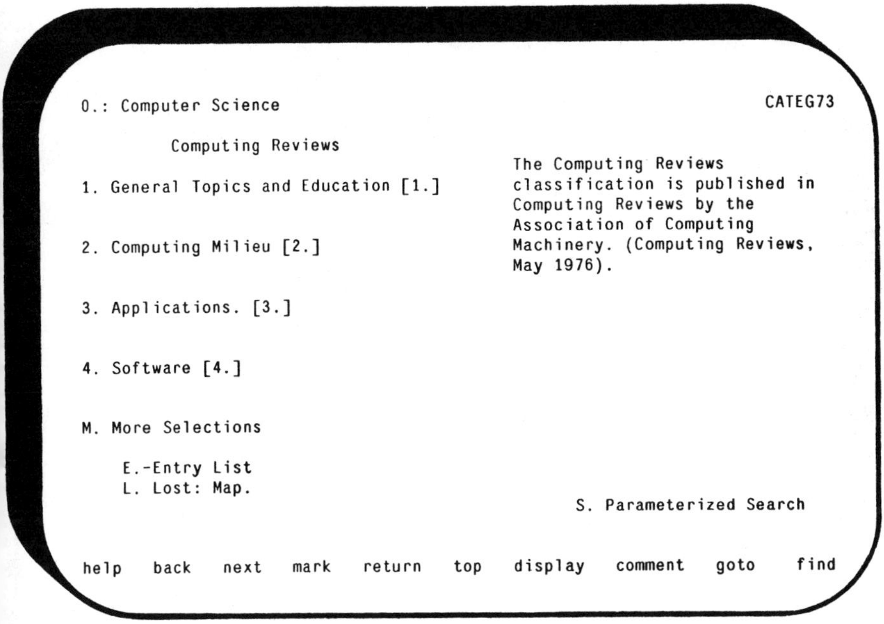

```
0.: Computer Science                                                CATEG73

        Computing Reviews
                                          The Computing Reviews
1. General Topics and Education [1.]      classification is published in
                                          Computing Reviews by the
                                          Association of Computing
2. Computing Milieu [2.]                  Machinery. (Computing Reviews,
                                          May 1976).

3. Applications. [3.]


4. Software [4.]


M. More Selections

     E.-Entry List
     L. Lost: Map.
                                          S. Parameterized Search


help    back    next    mark    return    top    display    comment    goto    find
```

Figure 3

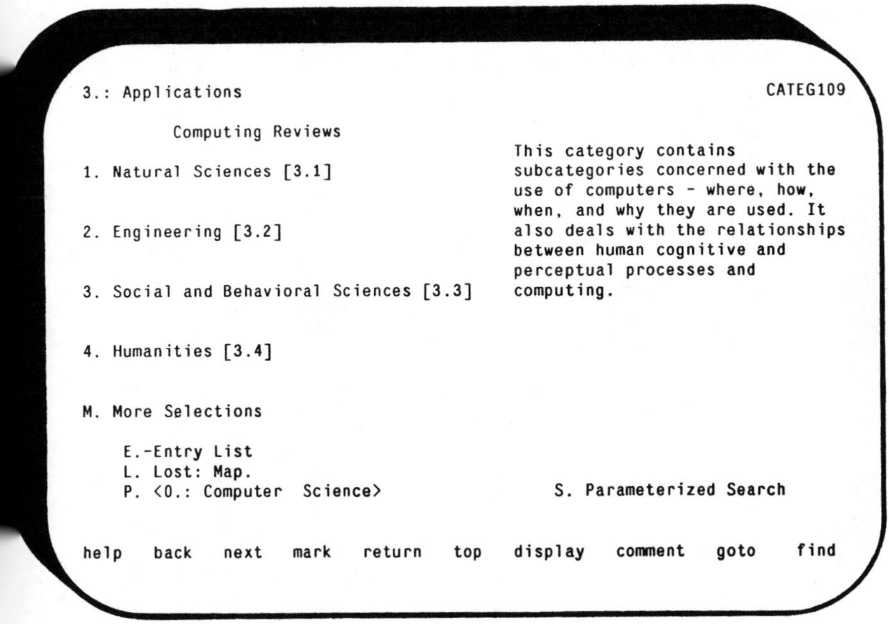

```
3.: Applications                                                    CATEG109

        Computing Reviews
                                          This category contains
1. Natural Sciences [3.1]                 subcategories concerned with the
                                          use of computers - where, how,
                                          when, and why they are used. It
2. Engineering [3.2]                      also deals with the relationships
                                          between human cognitive and
                                          perceptual processes and
3. Social and Behavioral Sciences [3.3]   computing.


4. Humanities [3.4]


M. More Selections

     E.-Entry List
     L. Lost: Map.
     P. <0.: Computer  Science>           S. Parameterized Search


help    back    next    mark    return    top    display    comment    goto    find
```

Figure 4

```
3.: Applications                                                    CATEG108

    Computing Reviews
                                        This category contains
1. Management Data Processing [3.5]     subcategories concerned with the
                                        use of computers - where, how,
                                        when, and why they are used. It
2. Artificial Intelligence [3.6]        also deals with the relationships
                                        between human cognitive and
                                        perceptual processes and
3. Information Retrieval [3.7]           computing.


4. Real-Time Systems [3.8]


M. More Selections

    E.-Entry List
    L. Lost: Map.
    P. <O.: Computing Review>           S. Parameterized Search


help   back   next   mark   return   top   display   comment   goto   find
```

Figure 5

```
3.6: Artificial Intelligence                                        CATEG76

    Computing Reviews
                                        This category contains
1. Induction and Hypothesis-Formation   subcategories pertaining to
   [3.61]                               induction and the formation of
                                        hypotheses; learning and
2. Learning and Adaptive Systems [3.62] inductive systems; pattern
                                        recognition; problem solving;
                                        simulation of natural systems;
3. Pattern Recognition [3.63]           theory of heuristic methods,
                                        and general and miscellaneous
                                        subjects within the broad area
4. Problem Solving [3.64]               of artificial intelligence, or
                                        the machine simulation and
                                        modeling of human functions,
M. More Selections                      particularly human
                                        intelligence.
    E. Entry List
    L. Lost: Map.
    P. <3.: Applications; >             S. Parameterized Search


help   back   next   mark   return   top   display   comment   goto   find
```

Figure 6

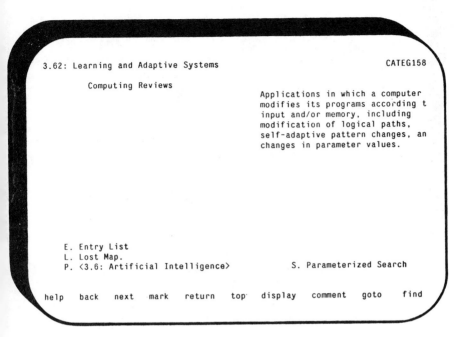

Figure 7

Intelligence, he would select option E. With an interest in learning systems, the user selects option 2, and the goal category frame has been reached (fig. 7).

There are no subcategories to Learning and Adaptive Systems. The user has reached a terminal frame in the classification hierarchy. The entry list (fig. 8) is displayed by selecting the E option. Along with the list of entries, this frame contains a pointer back to the category frame leading to the entry list (option R), and options to move back and forth through the entry list (option M and option P, which is not shown). This is just one form of indexing provided by BROWSE. In addition, the autogeneration of hierarchical and alphabetical indexes has been added.

The user decides that entry 6 looks interesting. Selecting that option, the frame in figure 9 is displayed. This frame provides the basic information about the article in question. The user may find additional information about the authors by selecting options A or B. If the user wants information about the Computer Science Department at Carnegie-Mellon University, he may get it by selecting option I. In all three cases, a list of entries associated with the author or institution will be available. The user can gain additional information about the symposim in which this article

```
3.62: Learning and Adaptive Systems                                    ENTRY89

1.  EG -- A case study in problem solving with king and pawn endings;
    Perdue, C.; Symposium or Conference Paper;
2.  Encoding knowledge in partitioned networks; Hendrix, Gary G.; Technical
    Report;
3.  Experiences in evaluation with BKG--A program that plays backgammon;
    Berliner, H.; Symposium or Conference Paper;
4.  Inference in the conceptual dependency paradigm: a personal history;
    Schank, Roger C.;
5.  Knowledge acquisition from structural descriptions; Hayes-Roth, F.;
    Symposium or Conference Paper;
6.  Knowledge-guided learning of structural descriptions; Fox, M. S.;
    Symposium or Conference Paper;
7.  Models of learning systems; Buchanan, Bruce G.;

8.  On fuzzy resolution; Aronson, Alan R.; Technical Report;


M. More Entries                                        R. Root Category

help  back  next  mark  return  top  display  comment  goto  find
```

Figure 8

```
                    Symposium

Knowledge-guided learning of structural descriptions


A. Fox, M.S.                          B. Reddy, D. R.
I. Computer Science Dept.
   Carnegie-Mellon University
   Pittsburgh, Pennsylvania

Page number:

F. Proceedings of the Fifth International Joint Conference on Artificial
     Intelligence


                         1. Acronyms and Keywords.
                         2. Abstract.
                         3. Circulation Information.
                         4. Alternate Category.

help  back  next  mark  return  top  display  comment  goto  find
```

Figure 9

appeared by selecting option F. Along with information about the symposium, a list of all articles will be provided. Finally, there is a set of options that provides additional information about the current entry. Option 1 will provide a list of acronyms and keywords. The keywords are organized as a list of options. If the user wants to see what other entries in the database share a keyword, he can select that keyword. The second option provides the abstract to the paper. The third option provides circulation information about the entry in the library. The fourth option leads to a list of categories under which the current article has been classified. These categories are options that point back into the classification hierarchy.

By selecting option 2, the user can view the abstract of the paper (fig. 10). The user decides that he wants to see additional information on M.S. Fox. By selecting option A in figure 10, he moves to a frame giving some information about the author (fig. 11). Options are provided for linearly moving through the author list ($<$,$>$) and going to the author index frame ($\uparrow$). By selecting option 1, the user is led to a frame listing all of Fox's articles that are currently in the database (fig. 12). Seeing nothing of additional interest, the user now decides to see Fox's other areas of interest (fig. 13).

```
SYMPOSIU                    Abstract

Knowledge-guided learning of structural descriptions

              A. Fox, M.S.
              B. Reddy, D. R.

We demonstrate how the use of domain dependent knowledge can reduce the
combinatorics of learning structural descriptions, using as an example the
creation of alternative pronunciations from examples of spoken words.
Briefly, certain learning problems (Winston, 1970; Fox & Hayes-Roth, 1976)
can be solved by presenting to a learning program exemplars (training
data) representative of a class. The program constructs a characteristic
representation (CR) of the class that best fits the training data.
Learning can be viewed as search in the space of representations. Applied
to complex domains the search is highly combinatorial due to the: 1)
Number of alternative CRs. 2) Size of training set. 3) Size of the
exemplars.



help    back    next    mark    return    top    display    comment    goto    find
```

Figure 10

```
                    Mark S. Fox                                    author1

NAME:   Mark S. Fox

ADDRESS:
   Computer Science Department
   Carnegie-Mellon University
   Pittsburgh, Pennsylvania 15213

DATE OF BIRTH:   9 May 1952



                    1.   Publications.

                    2.   Research interests.



    <. Previous author      ↑. Authors with initial F      >. Next author

help    back    next    mark    return    top    display    comment    goto    find
```

Figure 11

```
Publications:   Mark S. Fox                                        author2


   1.   Knowledge-Guided Learning of Structural Descriptions; Symposium paper.

   2.   Maximal Consistent Interpretations of Errorful Data in Hierarchically
        Modelled Domains; Symposium paper.









                                                    ↑. Root Frame

help    back    next    mark    return    top    display    comment    goto    find
```

Figure 12

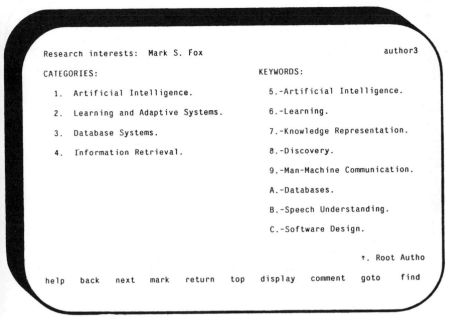

Figure 13

Also interested in information retrieval, the user selects option 4. This puts him back into the classification hierarchy (fig. 14). He may now continue browsing in that area. If the user has managed to get lost, there is the "lost map" option L. By selecting that option, the user can get a global view of the classification hierarchy that surrounds the current category (fig. 15). Surrounding categories can be reached by selecting any of the options.

Browsing and Searching

The BROWSE system relies on browsing as its primary method of database access. However, there are many times when parameterized search is desired. The user may already know exactly what he is looking for and should not have to move through the network of frames to get there.

The BROWSE system includes the ability to specify searches. As was shown in figure 2, each category frame in the current system has an option that allows the user to specify a parameterized search. The parameterized search differs from searches in normal PS-based systems in the following ways:

```
3.7: Information Retrieval                                          CATEG164

      Computing Reviews
                                          This category embraces
1. Content Analysis [3.71]                subcategories concerned with the
                                          systematic computer analysis,
                                          organization, storage, recovery,
2. Evaluation of Systems [3.72]           and dissemination of data.


3. File maintenance [3.73]


4. Searching [3.74]


M. More Selections

     E. Entry List
     L. Lost: Map.
     P. <3.: Applications; >                        S. Parameterized Search


help   back   next   mark   return   top   display   comment   goto   find
```

Figure 14

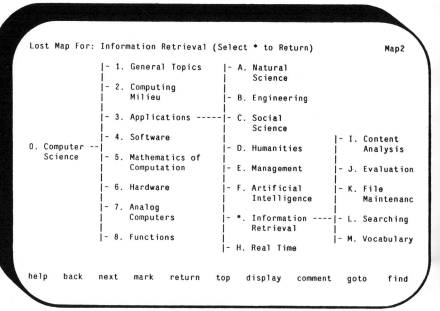

Figure 15

1. The search that is initiated is context-dependent. The user may browse through the classification hierarchy until he finds the area in which he is interested. When he initiates a search at that point, only entries classified under that category will be searched. Thus, if the user selected the "parameterized search" option at the frame for Artificial Intelligence, the procedure would only search entries directly classified under Artificial Intelligence and entries classified under all of the subcategories to Artificial Intelligence.

2. When the results of the search are returned to the user, he is able to browse through the list of found entries. He may also browse outside the list of satisfied entries (follow any link). The current search procedure returns a list of frames in the system that satisfy the search parameters. An additional set of options are provided that allow the user to move through the list. The list can be viewed as an additional classification structure. Thus, the user can make full use of the browsing capacity of the system.

The ability to combine browsing and searching reduces the problem with parameterized searches of not finding all the entries in which the user is interested. Often, closely related entries are not returned by the search. If the user is allowed to browse throughout the network, he can often find the entries related to the list of returned entries.

Measuring the Efficacy of the BROWSE System

We have shown what using the BROWSE system is like. Its purpose is to provide naïve users browsing access to information. Its success rests on how well it adheres to the principles of interface, structure and category perspicuity. Consider the interface factors described earlier:

1. *Time*: The search heuristics described earlier are the primary functions. They are provided by selecting an option in order to transfer to another frame. Frame change is rapid. Hence, the time it takes to accomplish a browsing task is small. The response time of parameterized search depends on the machine, the operating system and the program.

2. *Errors*: Restricting control to option selection virtually eliminates the problem of incorrect commands. When a user makes an incorrect option selection, the "back," "return" and "goto" global pads provide sufficient recovery. If the user gets lost, the lost map frame provides sufficient context.

3. *Learning*: The single most important control construct to be learned is option selection. This is a simple task to learn. Any other instruction is provided by frame text.

4. *Functionality*: Search heuristics are embedded in options. Other functions such as parameterized search are also provided by options.
5. *Recall*: The primary command to be remembered is option selection. Instruction is usually provided by the text of each frame. And the "help" global pad provides access to general instruction frames from every frame.
6. *Concentration*: The concentration required of the user is dependent upon the task. This example use of ZOG records the sequence of frames visited by the user so that the list may be displayed and reviewed. Nevertheless, complex searches may require the user to remember the nonlinear topology of the subnet visited. The difficulty of remembering spatial orientation results in the feeling of being lost. The problem is being studied,[6] and a number of approaches for dealing with it include the dynamic construction and display of maps of subnets visited by the user.[7]
7. *Fatigue*: Rapid response results in the system waiting for the user, not vice versa. Hence, the user does not tire from waiting for results.

Structure perspicuity is maintained in three ways: (1) each category lists its subcategories and also has a link to its supracategories, thus displaying a part of the categorization structure to the user; (2) the user can move through the structure quickly and easily, allowing assimilation of the structure; and (3) the "lost map" option (fig. 15) gives a more global view of the categorization structure. Category perspicuity is partially solved by providing a definition on each category frame. The user can also learn categories by example; he can quickly access all the entries in a particular category. As a system for naïve users, BROWSE appears to satisfy the principles well. Coupled with parameterized search capability, it provides a powerful system for public access to information.

Building BROWSE Systems

The BROWSE system is composed of two separate systems. There is a display system called ZOG and a system that is used to create the frame-structured database called the BROWSE System Software.

The ZOG System

The BROWSE system was designed to use ZOG, developed at Carnegie-Mellon University by Robertson and others, as its display system.[8] ZOG has its roots in the University of Vermont's PROMIS system.[9] To understand the philosophy of BROWSE, one must understand the philosophy of ZOG. ZOG is a rapid-response, large-network, menu-selection system for man-machine communication. A ZOG user sits in front of a terminal on which a frame is displayed. The frame consists of some text and a set of options. At the discretion of the user, an option is selected and almost instantaneously a new frame is displayed. The process then starts again. ZOG's basic features are:

1. *Rapid response*: When a user selects an option that leads to another frame, the next frame should appear fast enough so that the user does not feel he is waiting for the system. A user must feel free to explore surrounding frames without concerning himself with the time it takes to display each frame.
2. *Simple selection*: The act of selection should be a simple unitary gesture. At the present time, there are two forms of selection available: (1) single character input from the keyboard, and (2) a touch screen.
3. *Large network*: The network should be large enough to provide most of the information needed by the user.
4. *Frame simplicity*: The frame display should be kept simple. The user should be able to assimilate the information contained in the frame quickly. The idea of frame simplicity has led to the development of frames that contain a small amount of text and up to five or six options. This is not necessarily true of frames developed for the BROWSE system, where the simplicity comes from the very structured nature of the information. Although a large amount of information may be displayed on a single frame, the information desired by the user can still be assimilated quickly.
5. *Transparency*: The user should be able to understand exactly what the system is doing and what he needs to do to gain additional information. At no point should the user feel that he has lost control of the system.
6. *Communication agent*: ZOG has been designed to act as a communication agent between a user and another system. As a communication agent, ZOG presents commands to the user in a simple format, as well as an explanation of what the command will do. When the user makes a selection, ZOG sends the more complex set of commands to the other system for processing. This facility is used by the BROWSE system for the parameterized search interface.
7. *External definition*: Unlike many menu-selection systems, ZOG-nets are databases which are independent of and external to the ZOG system.

The basic philosophy of ZOG is that a menu-selection system can be an effective communication system if the user can move around in the system quickly, and if there is a large network available to meet the user's needs.

A menu-selection system allows the user almost complete knowledge of what is occurring in the system whenever he selects an option. It also allows for related information to be located nearby (by placing a link between related frames). Menu-selection systems normally have a disadvantage in the time it takes to move from one frame to another. This is solved by the fast response of the ZOG system. Another characteristic of many menu-selection systems is that the same information is provided to all users, regardless of their needs or expertise. In ZOG, different paths would be provided for each level of user. The naïve user would get more information about what he is doing, while the expert user would be presented with only the frames needed to perform the task.

The BROWSE System Software

A major problem with menu-based systems is the creation of the menus. Experiments with the ZOG system have shown that the average rate of frame creation is approximately five frames per hour.[10] Given a database that contains in excess of 1 million frames, it becomes clear that some machine-aided creation mechanism is needed.

The BROWSE system solution to that problem was to create a software package external to the display system (ZOG) to create the database network. The software is designed to translate a database into a frame database. The reasons for using an external database and a translation system are:

1. To allow for the modification of the frame formats. The design of frame formats and network structures may change, requiring the frame database to be recreated. ZOG does not provide facilities for the automatic modification of frames and structure.
2. To allow for the creation of different networks for different display types. At the present time the BROWSE system runs only on a standard 24-by-80-character display terminal. A completely different frame structure would be used for a high-resolution display terminal.
3. To allow for parameterized searches. It would be cumbersome to carry out the parameterized search within the frame network. Thus, the search is carried out by a separate program that accesses the original database.

The BROWSE system is a set of software that provides the following capabilities: the ability to create a record database and new record types with access and search software; interactive programs to query data-entry personnel for new entries for the database; interactive definition of frame formats; interactive definition of record linkages which define how frames are linked in the frame network; and frame creation, by combining: (1) a new record in the database, (2) a frame format description, and (3) a linkage specification; to produce new frames and updated frames (e.g., index frames), with the proper option links, for the frame database. Hence, the total effect of the software is to translate a record database into a browsable frame database for naïve users.

Recognizing that the visual format of frames is important to the overall acceptability of the system, we designed the frame format description language to provide a variety of layout capabilities. The frame format describes:

1. the information to be placed in the frame (fields of a record),
2. the placement of the information in windows on the screen,
3. the information actually necessary to create the frame,
4. the options to appear in the frame, and
5. the type of frame to which each option may lead.

The frame format consists of (in increasing order of complexity): (1) window descriptions, (2) option descriptions, (3) fill descriptions, (4) group descriptions, and (5) index descriptions.

The window description (WD) is the basic unit of the frame format. The WD includes information describing a two-dimensional area into which text will be placed. The WD contains a starting coordinate for the window. This position is relative to the group that accesses the window. The WD also contains a minimum and maximum length and width of the window.

The option description (OD) contains information that relates to options in the ZOG frame. Included in that information is the selection character for the option, the touch area of the option (in case a pointing device is available), the text to be included as part of the option text, the frame type to which the option leads, and a WD that is to be used to hold the text of the option.

The fill description (FD) describes the information (fields) from the database that is to be used to fill a window. The FD also points to a WD. In evaluating an FD, the system retrieves the contents of the fields in the current record. The FD contains information on what to do if the contents of a field are null, as well as the text to place before and after the text found. All the text specified is concatenated and then placed in the window. Also included in the FD is information describing the size, typeface and font to be used in displaying the text (for use with a high-resolution display), as well as commands describing how to display the text in the window (centered, flush right, flush left, filled).

The group description (GD) is one of the two major units of the frame format. A GD combines a set of FDs (and possibly index description, or an ID) into a single logical unit. The GD points to a set of FDs. If the GD is describing an option, then the GD will also point to an OD. The GD also contains an absolute anchor point for the group. An anchor defines the root position of the group on the frame. The starting positions provided by the WDs and referenced by the GD are relative to that anchor point. The anchor point of the group can be set relative to other groups (i.e., the anchor point of group X can be placed one line below the last line used by group Y).

The other major unit of the frame format is the index description (ID). Associated with every category frame is an option to a list of entries. That list is a linear index, ordered alphabetically by title, to all the entries in that category. One of the major problems with an evolving system is that the indexes to the system must constantly be rebuilt. The ID has been included in the frame format to allow the system to create indexes mechanically. The system is capable of creating a variety of index types (linear, hierarchical, alphabetical). The ID points to two sets of GDs. The first set refers to groups that are used as titles to the index. The second set is used for actually creating the index. The ID also contains information on how to form the list of entries to be used in creating the index.

Conclusion

The application of computer technology to information and library systems has created a vista of opportunities. The possibility of a revolution in how information is stored, accessed and manipulated beckoned, but the actual introduction of technology produced as many problems as it solved. These systems are difficult to learn and use, creating a serious barrier to the naïve user. Second, some researchers were clouded in their thinking by the way they used information systems. They were unable to see beyond their current horizon, thus asserting that computers could not provide certain styles of interaction such as browsing.[11] The main effect of this was a plethora of research in the parameterized mode of search. The combination of the BROWSE and ZOG systems provides a radically different approach to the access and display of information. BROWSE and ZOG provide an integrated browsing and parameterized approach to searching databases, while utilizing an interface that is simple and clear for even the naïve user.

ACKNOWLEDGMENTS

This research was sponsored by the Office of Naval Research under contract No. N00014-76-0874, and, in part, by the Defense Advanced Research Projects Agency (DOD), Arpa Order No. 3597, monitored by the Air Force

Avionics Laboratory Contract 533615-78-C-1551. The authors wish to thank the people involved in the ZOG project for providing the important display component of the BROWSE system; also, special thanks to Earl Mounts, head of the Computer Science Browsing Room at Carnegie-Mellon University, for his help in developing the BROWSE system.

REFERENCES

1. Fox, Mark S., and Palay, Andrew J. "The BROWSE System: An Introduction." *In* Roy D. Tally and Ronald R. Dueltgen, eds. *Information Choices and Policies: Proceedings of the ASIS Annual Meeting.* Vol. 16. White Plains, N.Y., Knowledge Industry, 1979, pp. 183-93; and _____ . "The BROWSE System: Phase II and Future Research." Pittsburgh, Pa., Computer Science Dept., Carnegie-Mellon University, 1979. (unpublished)

2. Fox, Mark S., et al. "The Automated Dictionary," *Computer* 13:35-48, July 1980.

3. Mylopolous, J., et al. "TORUS: Natural Language Understanding System for Data Management." In *Proceedings of the Fourth International Joint Conference on Artificial Intelligence* (Tbilisi, USSR, 1975). Cambridge, Mass., Artificial Intelligence Laboratory, 1975 pp. 414-21; Waltz, D. "Natural Language Access to Large Data Bases: An Engineering Approach." In *Proceedings,* op. cit., pp. 868-72; Sacerdoti, E.D. "Language Access to Distributed Data with Error Recovery." In *Proceedings of the Fifth International Joint Conference on Artificial Intelligence* (Cambridge, Mass., 1977). Pittsburgh, Carnegie-Mellon University, 1977; and Hayes-Roth, F., et al. "Understanding Speech in the Hearsay-II System." *In* Leonard Bolc, ed. *Speech Communication with Computers.* Munich, Macmillan, 1978, pp. 9-42.

4. Card, S.K., et al. "The Keystroke-Level Model for User Performance Time with Interactive Systems" (AIP Memo 122). Palo Alto, Calif., Xerox Palo Alto Research Center, 1979. (Report SSL-79-1)

5. Bates, Marcia J. "Factors Affecting Subject Catalog Search Success," *Journal of the ASIS* 28:161-69, May 1977.

6. Mantei, M. "Disorientation Behavior in Man-Computer Interfaces." Ph.D. diss., Annenberg School of Communications, University of Southern California, 1981.

7. Fox and Palay, "The BROWSE System: Phase II," op. cit.

8. Robertson, G., et al. "The ZOG Approach to Man-Machine Communication" (Technical Report). Carnegie-Mellon University, Dept. of Computer Science, 1979.

9. Shultz, J., et al. "An Initial Operational Problem Oriented Medical Record System—For Storage, Manipulation and Retrieval of Medical Data." In *AFIPS Conference Proceedings: National Computer Conference and Exposition.* Vol. 38. Montvale, N.J., AFIPS Press, 1971, pp. 765-77.

10. McCracken, Donald L., and Robertson, George G. "Editing Tools for ZOG, a Highly Interactive Man-Machine Interface." *In* Institute of Electrical and Electronics Engineers. *ICC '76: International Conference on Communications.* New York, IEEE, 1979, pp. 22.7.1-7.5.

11. Myers, Charles A. *Computers in Knowledge-Based Fields.* Cambridge, Mass., MIT Press, 1970.

ADDITIONAL REFERENCES

"Categories of the Computing Sciences," *Computing Reviews* 17:172-98, May 1976.

Fedida, S. "Viewdata—An Interactive Information Medium for the General Public Using the Telephone Network." In *IBC 76: International Broadcasting Convention* (IEE Conference Pub. No. 145). London, Institution of Electrical Engineers, 1976, pp. 107-12.

GREGG VANDERHEIDEN
Director
TRACE Research and Development Center
University of Wisconsin

Modifying and Designing Computer Terminals to Allow Access by Handicapped Individuals

INTRODUCTION

For handicapped individuals, the primary problems in dealing with computer terminals fall into two categories: manipulation of the keyboard, and dealing with the information displayed. Manipulation problems are usually experienced by individuals with physical handicaps, including the elderly. The second category, dealing with the information presented on the tube, is a problem for both blind individuals and individuals who may have trouble dealing with more complex information. For blind individuals, the problem is primarily one of presenting information in the wrong sensory mode. The complexity of the information display, however, may also be a barrier to some sighted users, such as young children, people with low vision, some elderly individuals, and individuals with varying degrees of language or cognitive disability. Deaf persons generally do not experience any difficulty in dealing with terminals unless there is significant and nonredundant information presented auditorially, either with speech or through beeps and other audible cues. With systems designed to function in libraries these are generally not significant problems, since the systems are usually designed to operate silently or with a minimum of auditory cueing.

In this paper, each of the three areas of handicap—visual, physical and cognitive—will be explored, along with the different approaches which have been used to provide access to textual information. Some of the approaches are simple; others are complex. The following section of the paper will then examine the practical constraints to be considered in designing public access data processing terminals. These include considerations and constraints experienced by both the user and the manufacturer. Finally, the paper will reexamine the various solution strategies presented in the first section in light of these practical considerations and constraints. Practical, low-cost, minimum modification approaches which best meet the constraints of manufacturers and users will be identified.

Strategies for the Visually Impaired

Solution strategies for individuals with visual impairments fall into three basic categories: (1) visual enlargement; (2) tactile displays; and (3) auditory displays. There are several ways of visually enlarging the output display. One technique is to expand the visual image on the display electronically. This gives a "zoom" effect, making the images on the screen larger, but means that a smaller portion of the screen is seen at any one time. A second approach is to use a separate magnifying lens. This solution has the advantage that the display itself does not need to be modified in any special fashion. The magnifying lens can be positioned in front of the display either mechanically or manually, and moved by the individual to scan the information on the page. This same effect can be achieved at a much higher cost by using a magnifying lens on a closed-circuit television camera.

The second approach for visually impaired individuals is a tactile display. While the first approach is intended mostly for individuals with impaired vision, the second approach is intended primarily for individuals with no vision. Tactile displays take basically two forms. The first is an actual representation of the characters themselves. The Opticon is an example of this approach. The Opticon is an aid which has a small camera, about the size of a pack of gum. This camera is connected to the main unit of the Opticon, which is about the size of a cassette tape recorder. The individual moves the camera over the printed letters or the characters on the television screen, and the Opticon reproduces, on the fingertips of the individual's other hand, the shapes of the letters or characters being scanned by the camera. In this way, the individual actually "feels" the various printed characters, and can read them directly. This approach has the advantage that an individual trained in the use of the Opticon can read most types of printed or displayed materials without special adapters. The second form of tactile display involves use of the Braille system. With Braille, each character or group of characters is represented by a pattern of raised dots. These can be punched into paper or presented using dynamic Braille displays, which have little pins that move up and down. Dynamic Braille displays are usually single-cell or single-line displays, since a full-page dynamic Braille display would be extremely expensive.

The third approach to information display for visually impaired individuals is the use of auditory displays. This approach can be used with both blind and visually impaired individuals. With this approach, the information displayed visually is also spoken. Talking terminals of this sort are most effective for transferring bulk text. Selection menus and complex visually oriented displays are more difficult to comprehend if simply read from the screen. This is particularly true when two or three columns are displayed. Therefore, special processing of the information is usually required, rather than simply having the user read the information off the screen one line at a time (which would give the first entry on each of the three columns, then the second entry on each column, etc.). This approach is almost useless with graphic or charted information, as is the dynamic Braille approach. The only approaches which are useful at all for graphic or charted information are the enlarged screen and the direct tactile translation (i.e., Opticon).

Strategies for Physically Handicapped Individuals

For physically handicapped individuals the problem is more complex, due to the greater variety of physical disabilities. As a result, a wide variety of approaches exists to match not only the varying needs and disabilities, but also the varying residual control these individuals may have. This section provides an overview of some of the basic and more applicable approaches for use with data terminals.

All of the techniques can be broken down into two fundamental approaches. The first approach is *direct selection*. Any technique where the individual directly points to the various choices (e.g., using a typewriter keyboard or pointing to selections directly on the terminal screen) is an example of direct selection. The second basic approach is *scanning*. The scanning technique is used wherever the individual is unable to point for himself. With this approach, items are presented sequentially to the individual. When the desired item is reached, the individual signals by operating some type of switch. Thus, the scanning approach is essentially "selection in time," while the direct selection approach could be called "selection in space." The scanning approach is much slower and more cumbersome than the direct selection approach, and is therefore usually used only in situations where direct selection is not possible.

Direct Selection Techniques

Direct selection techniques can take a wide variety of forms, but all essentially provide the individual with some mechanism for pointing. These techniques may take advantage of whatever body part over which the individual has best control, including finger, hand, arm, leg, knee, foot, head, or eye. In some cases, the individual can point directly to the particular item (see fig. 1). In other cases, some type of pointer such as a headstick, finger pointer, etc., may be used (see fig. 2). A very powerful new technique which has received much more application recently is the use of optical pointers. With this technique, an individual points using a beam of light. This approach has the advantage that the "length" of the beam automatically adjusts to the distance necessary to reach the item indicated. This allows the individual to exert much less physical control. It also permits the individual to stay in his best position, rather than having to lean in one direction or another to reach his choice, as he would with a mechanical pointer. This ability to maintain optimal position can greatly increase an individual's pointing capabilities. Individuals with good discrete pointing skills can generally use these various techniques directly. Other individuals can use these techniques to point, but their pointing motions may be mixed with erratic or involuntary jerking motions. The individual may not be able to hold his hand, finger, or pointer still over a single selection, or may not be able to press a single switch. In these cases, the "auto-monitoring technique" can be used. This approach has an "averaging" effect which allows an individual to point, even shakily, to an item, and have the system determine which item he or she is trying to indicate. Even if the individual makes occasional wrong selections, the system can ignore these false signals and pick out the desired target of the individual's pointing.

Most recently, research has begun into the use of eyes for direct pointing. Using the eyes to point is very difficult for a number of reasons. It isn't possible to attach something easily to the eye to use either as a pointer or as a reference for sensing eye position. Optical methods for determining eye position have been used, but generally these need to be individually calibrated, are sensitive to ambient light conditions or are sensitive to position and orientation. Many of the eye position-sensing systems also measure only eye position with respect to the head. In order to tell where the individual is looking, one must determine where the head is with respect to the target. These two pieces of information (eye position and head position) then need to be integrated in order to determine the position of the gaze. Although this approach is difficult to implement, its potential is great, especially for aids which are custom-fit to the individual. Practical implementation of this technique with custom aids is, however, at least several years away. Use of this system for public access terminals, where it would need to be self-calibrating and able to work with a wide variety of individuals, is farther away yet.

With these various techniques, it is usually possible to find some mechanism through which the individual can point or indicate directly. If

Figure 1. Direct selection by manual pointing

the individual can point directly, but only to a small number of items, then multisignal techniques such as encoding can be used (discussed later). For individuals who are unable to point at all, however, a scanning approach may be required.

Scanning Techniques

While direct selection techniques are methods where the individual himself points, scanning techniques are basically methods where something or someone else points for the individual. The individual then watches until the desired item is presented. At that time, he gives a signal of some type to indicate that the desired item has been reached. For an individual to be able to use this technique, he need only have some single motion which he can control. This can be a movement of any part of his body, or the cessation of movement. An eye blink, a look upward, a

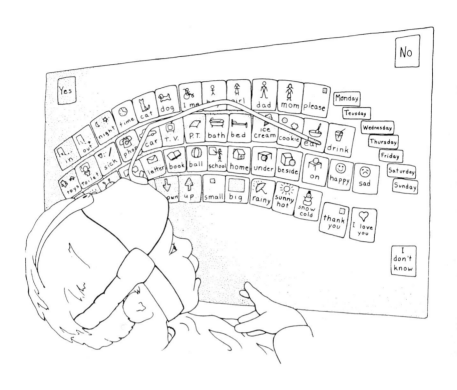

Figure 2. Direct selection by using a headstick

movement of the thumb, etc. are all acceptable movements which could be either observed or tapped using a switch. Because of this, scanning is an extremely powerful technique.

The disadvantages of the scanning approach is that it is much slower. This is especially true if the number of choices is large. If an individual must spell out information, for example, it can take a very long time to scan the alphabet, picking out each letter individually. The time required to transmit information in this manner ranges from long to excruciatingly long, depending upon the amount of information and the individual's response time.

One of the primary reasons for the extended time required to transfer information using the scanning approach is that the bulk of the time is spent displaying "wrong" choices. In order to accelerate the scanning process, therefore, several techniques have been developed to reduce the number of wrong choices presented. One method is the use of group/item scanning. With this technique, groups of items are first presented to the individual, until he gives a signal indicating that the desired item is in that group. The individual items within that group are then scanned individually until the desired item is reached. If a very large number of choices are possible, then a group/group/item approach can be used. The most popular forms of group/item scanning are row/column (or row/item) scanning and page/item scanning (see fig. 3).

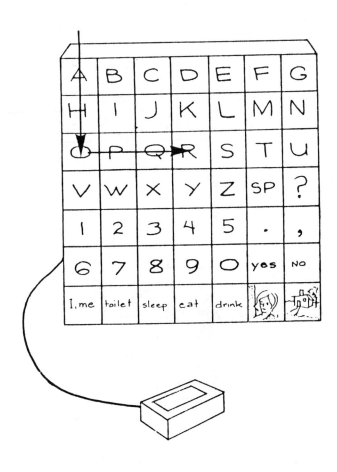

Figure 3a. Row-column scanning

A	B	C	D	E	F	G	H
I	J	K	L	M	N	O	P
Q	R	S	T	U	V	W	X
Y	Z	1	2	3	4	5	6
7	8	9	0	;	?	Space	Is
Are	To	What	Why	Go	The	For	Bath-room
Me	You	They	Mary	John	Mom	Dad	Eat
Drink	Sleep	Help	Sick	Time	Please	Thank you	Want

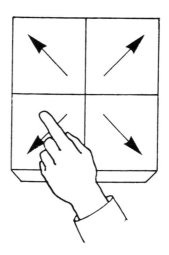

Figure 3b. Successive quartering

Another technique to reduce the number of wrong presentations is to arrange the items in order of frequency of use. Thus, the most used items are placed toward the front of the scanning routine, since they are more probably the next correct item. In cases where selections are used in a certain pattern, such as in English spelling, the most probable next letter will vary depending upon the preceding letter or letters selected. In such cases, the order of presentation can be changed after each selection to display the most probable next selection. This technique should be implemented with care, however, since it is sometimes more confusing to have the selection order change each time, causing the individual to take more time in his selection and thus losing some of the advantages of predictive scanning. Over long periods, however, the individual may be able to anticipate the changing displays so that this problem can be reduced or eliminated.

Encoding Techniques

Even with the above scanning acceleration techniques, the scanning approach is generally still considered to be a second choice to any type of direct selection technique. For situations where the individual can only select a small number of items, however, the total selection space (total number of possible selections) can be expanded by using what have been termed *encoding techniques.*

Encoding techniques constitute only one part of a larger category of techniques which use multiple signals from the user to increase the "selection space" that an individual would have with direct selection, or decrease the "selection time" of an individual using the scanning approach. Some multisignal techniques for scanning were discussed above, such as group/-item scanning.

A parallel to the group/item concept in scanning is two-number encoding or group/item indication using direct selection. With this technique, an individual who is able to point to only ten numbers could quickly select from 100 items by simply pointing to a pair of numbers. One can think of this either as indicating a number from zero to ninety-nine, or as selecting one of ten groups, and then one of ten items within the group. In both cases, the time and movements involved are identical. The major difference is in how the information is displayed. There are advantages to either approach, although the pairing of individual numbers with individual choices is almost always the superior approach due to the reduced amount of visual scanning and processing necessary. These individually coded selections can then be grouped if desired or appropriate (see fig. 4).

Thus, the advantage of the encoding technique is that it can be used to provide an individual capable of relatively little movement or accuracy

12 A	24 H	36 O	52 V
13 B	25 I	41 P	53 W
14 C	26 J	42 Q	54 X
15 D	31 K	43 R	56 Y
16 E	32 L	45 S	61 Z
21 F	34 M	46 T	62 SP
23 G	35 N	51 U	63 ;

Figure 4a.
Two-movement encoding

Figure 4b. Scan encoding

with the ability to point to a large number of items. Ten widely spaced keys, for instance, could be used in a two-movement encoding technique to select any key on a keyboard or selection panel. Three-movement encoding would allow one to specify any of 1000 keys or selections.

Thus, it is possible to provide individuals having a wide variety of physical handicaps with access to systems of any level of complexity. Techniques exist, in fact, which can allow any individual, no matter how severe the physical handicap, to control information-processing systems. Choice of the appropriate technique will depend upon the application, the amount of information required, the variety of individuals who will be using the system, and the amount of modification which can be reasonably expected. For custom, personal aids, these constraints would be much different than for public access computer or information-access terminals.

Cognitive Considerations

In addition to the physical and sensory considerations, systems need to be designed which can be used by individuals having varying cognitive and language capabilities. Some design considerations are necessary to ensure that the systems can be used by younger children or by elderly individuals. In other cases, modifications might be implemented to allow the systems to be more easily used by individuals with specific language or cognitive processing difficulties resulting form stroke, injury or other conditions.

Typical considerations in this area would be: (1) use of simple visual displays; (2) use of large, plainly-marked input panels; (3) use of a minimal number of keys and options—use of a hidden-option approach; and (4) use of simple categorical presentations. Most of these are self-explanatory. The hidden-option approach allows the system to support faster and more efficient data entry approaches for individuals who are familiar with the system, while providing a perhaps slower but much more straightforward data entry or retrieval procedure for other individuals. Two techniques for achieving this are: (1) to make a number of the options invisible so that they can be called up, but are not necessarily displayed to the novice; (2) to have prompted and nonprompted input sequences.

Practical Considerations and Constraints

From the previous section, it can be seen that the problem of access lies not in finding a method to provide access to these systems for individuals with severe physical or sensory handicaps. There are a large number of techniques which can provide very effective interface approaches for individuals with almost any type of physical or sensory handicap. The problem instead is one of finding a practical, cost-efficient and effective method for providing this access.

User Constraints

Design constraints fall into two categories: user constraints and manufacturer/distribution constraints. The user constraints will vary somewhat depending upon the application for which the special terminals will be used. In general, however, there are four basic user constraints, especially for public access terminals. The system and modifications must be: (1) obvious, (2) easy to learn, (3) easy to set up or connect with, and (4) reliable and easy to maintain. The first two are, of course, general rules; they apply not only to handicapped individuals, but to the population as a whole. The third is appropriate mainly in terms of use by handicapped individuals. Adaptation of the systems for these individuals should not take even a few minutes nor require an engineer. Librarians are not going to have the time to hook up each individual as he comes in, or to remove or put away equipment carefully after each use. If the method for interfacing to the system is simple, it will be used. If the system is at all complex, however, it will generally not be connected or maintained. If, in addition, the system requires any significant amount of extra training on the part of the library staff or the handicapped individuals who will use it, the changes of it being utilized are further decreased.

Maintenance is another important area of concern. Will adding these capabilities make the system prone to breakage? A system which is in one piece, keyboard and display together, will be much more reliable and need less maintenance than a system which is built around many separate, interconnected units. No matter how simple and firm the connectors, they are always susceptible to being pulled and pushed, knocked, hit, and jammed. Systems with multiple components from different sources also make it much more difficult to maintain the system. Extra mechanical adaptations, which would be in the way for nonhandicapped users and therefore removed and replaced with each use, are also much more susceptible to damage and loss. Replacement and maintenance of modified systems is a very serious problem, and becomes more serious as modifications increase in number and complexity.

Manufacturer and Support Constraints

In addition to the constraints mentioned above, there are a number of considerations with regard to the manufacture and maintenance of the systems. One of the first concerns of the manufacturer is cost. If the basic terminal costs x, how much more would the terminal cost with the modifications included? How much would it cost to research and develop these extra capabilities as a part of the basic design? If a library would pay x for the system, how much more might they pay if these features were added?

Time is also a very important factor for the manufacturer. The goal is to deliver a finished product to the public as quickly as possible. Will these adaptations mean another six to twelve months on the drawing board? If the system is already in production, can these adaptations simply be added to the system, or will completed terminals have to be reworked? If they must be redesigned, what happens to the terminals and the systems already out in the field?

Documentation and training force up costs and add to the time involved. It costs an incredible amount of money to create user manuals. Will these special-purpose features mean additional training materials and training time for library staff? How much extra training will be necessary for the manufacturer's representatives? How will this affect the cost of the overall systems?

Practical Solution Strategies

All of these factors are very real, and must be taken into account when considering modifications of systems to optimize their use by individuals with handicaps. For this reason, it is not sufficient simply to develop or describe techniques for providing access for handicapped individuals. Instead, it is necessary to tackle the much more difficult task of determining techniques which can not only provide effective methods for access, but which also can minimize the cost, maintenance and other aspects necessary for the techniques to be practical and implementable. With these constraints in mind, one can examine the various strategies discussed earlier. Of particular interest will be the identification of those strategies which can best accommodate the various constraints.

Strategies for the Visually Impaired
The first technique discussed was visual enlargement. Displays can be made larger through a number of electronic techniques, but these are all technically complicated and would involve extensive modification of the circuitry in the terminal. Moreover, magnifying the display in this fashion only permits the user to view a portion of the overall display. If all of the letters were made twice as high (and twice as wide), for instance, the user would only be able to see one-fourth of the original screen at a time. To see the entire screen, he would have to look at four different displays or be provided with some type of electronic "moving window" which would allow him, in effect, to move around on the original screen. This, again, is expensive and somewhat disorienting visually.

Use of an optical magnifier for this function, however, would provide the same basic capability at much reduced cost. Essentially, the terminal could be outfitted either with a large magnifier which would sit in front of the screen and allow the individual to see the entire screen magnified by some factor, or with a large hand-held magnifying lens which could be attached to the terminal or desk with a chain. Maintenance, construction and replacement of these magnifiers would be very simple. Many libraries already have magnifying lenses of this sort, and visually impaired individuals are generally familiar with the use of such lenses.

The second general technique mentioned was the use of tactile displays. These displays are almost always very expensive, since they are designed using nonstandard technologies. In addition, these systems generally require extensive training to be used effectively, and therefore do not lend themselves easily for use with a public terminal. Finally, since the systems rarely use full-page displays, some modification of the display format may be necessary to provide an easily comprehensible tactile display. For these reasons, it would be difficult for terminal manufacturers to build any type of tactile display into their terminals. A better approach would be to provide an output port from the terminal. This alternative would both be inexpensive and provide a ready mechanism for individuals to connect their personal tactile displays. In addition, libraries that so desired could connect to these ports special tactile computer terminals designed specifically for a given population.

The questions surrounding the practicality of voice-output or talking terminals closely parallel the previous discussions. In general, it would be very difficult for computer terminal manufacturers or information retrieval system developers to design voice-output systems as accessories to an overall system. Auditory display of information usually needs to be done in a method quite different from visual displays of information. One major difference is that a visual display is essentially a parallel display of all of the information on the screen. An auditory display is a serial display of the information. Layout of the screen, the format of presentation, and the methods used to scan displays to select the desired information differ in large degree. For this reason, the best approach here, too, would be to provide a port to which individuals could connect their individual aids.

Another very simple and cost-effective strategy is to provide a composite video signal on an output jack. This would allow the system to have a second CRT display. That second display could be anything from a slightly larger television monitor with a moderate expansion of the display to a projected television screen. In this manner, one could theoretically have a terminal with a keyboard and a four-by-six-foot screen. With this technique, the entire screen can be expanded in size, not just a portion of it.

Computer video output is already provided on some terminals, and for other terminals would add as little as $3-$5 to the cost.

As with all of the techniques discussed here, the best overall approach to the problem of optimizing terminals for use by specific populations of handicapped individuals is to contact major centers for the visually impaired and to talk with professionals who are experts in the area of adaptation for this population. They can be provided with the specific constraints of the situation, and can offer guidance as to the most practical, cost-effective and useful approaches for that particular situation.

Strategies for Use by Physically Handicapped Individuals

As pointed out earlier, the most efficient and straightforward techniques are those of direct selection. For this reason, attention should first be turned to techniques which can be used to implement this type of approach. The first modification to be provided should be a keyboard guard or mask (see fig. 5). A keyguard or mask is simply a plate of plastic, wood or metal which fits over the keyboard and has holes drilled or punched in it directly above each of the keys. The purpose of the guard is to give the individual a surface on which he can rest and slide his hand without accidentally activating the keys. To operate individual keys, he simply moves his finger, thumb or dowel down through the holes (which are the same size as or slightly larger than the keys). Such keyboard guards can be made quite easily and inexpensively. IBM, for example, manufactures them for all of their typewriters and sells them for about ten dollars. Keyguards for public access terminals should be designed so that they can be easily attached or removed, to allow use of the terminals by nonhandicapped individuals as well. When in place, they should be firm. The space bar should be treated as any other key on the keyboard, except that three holes may be provided instead of one. A cutout the size of the entire space bar should *not* be made in the keyguard, since this usually results in a large number of inadvertent spaces by the individual.

Another approach is to provide alternate keyboards. These keyboards could be expanded and recessed (under a keyguard) to facilitate use by different handicapped individuals. This approach, however, is very expensive and would require the fabrication and fitting of various sizes and configurations of keyboards to accommodate different types of physical disabilities. Here again, a good approach is to provide an input connecter which would parallel the functions of the keyboard. Many handicapped individuals who require special keyboards have custom communication aids. With such aids, they could simply connect to the port, if it used a standard code (such as ASCII), and be able to duplicate *all* the functions of the keyboard.

Figure 5. Guarded keyboard

Another very powerful direct selection technique is the use of a light-beam pointer. This can be attached to the head, held in the hand, attached to a limb, etc., in order to provide an effective means of pointing. One technique for implementing the light-beam pointer is to use a long-range light pen coupled with a cursor on the terminal screen: the cursor moves to wherever the light beam points. Any system already configured to use a light pen could be easily modified to use this particular technique through software modifications and redesign of the light pen itself. This would allow for direct menu selection of items by individuals with fairly severe physical handicaps. It would also facilitate ease of use by elderly individuals or individuals prone to fatigue, for whom normal light pens may be difficult to use for extended periods of time; they could simply hold the light pen in their lap and point it at the various items on the screen. If a "keyboard" were provided at the bottom of the screen, individuals could use the light pen for typing in entries, as well as for selecting items from the menu. If the menu used up the entire screen, a white square in one corner of the screen could be used to allow the individual to switch from the menu display to a keyboard display to type in his messages. With this technique, the "auto-monitoring technique" described earlier could be used to allow individuals with less accurate pointing skills to use the system.

This latter technique could also be of value to nonhandicapped librarians and data-entry personnel. By simply clipping the light pen to the bow of their glasses, for example, they could use the light beam capability to cause the cursor to jump to different portions of the screen instantly, rather than having to use a slowly moving cursor to inch their way around the screen when filling out new entries. They would use the keyboard for normal data entry. The cursor can be moved simply by holding down a special key which activates the headpointer, allowing instant repositioning of the cursor anywhere on the screen.

For simple menu-type selection, a scanning routine can be implemented within the terminal. The only hardware modification necessary would be the addition of a miniature phone jack. The rest of the modification can be implemented as a rather simple addition to the selection algorithm. The actual scanning routine would be invisible to anybody using the terminal. The nonhandicapped user would make his selection using the keyboard or light pen in the normal fashion. The special scanning software routine needed by handicapped users would be triggered by a switch closure coming into the system through the miniature phone jack. At the first switch closure, a cursor scans the choices on the screen one at a time. This scanning process slowly decreases in speed until a second signal is received from the input jack. This second switch closure selects a particular item from the menu and also establishes a comfortable scanning rate. Subsequent switch closures would initiate and halt additional menu scans, always at the comfortable scan rate. Such a system should always include a method for confirming each selection to be sure that the individual selected the item actually wanted. This can best be accomplished by having the system scan two choices, such as CANCEL and CORRECT, after each selection until the individual selects one or the other. This scanning can be done at a fairly slow speed, since there are only two choices.

For larger numbers of choices, the linear technique described above can be extremely slow. In these cases, a group/item scanning approach or a scan/encode approach can be used, depending upon the method normally used for the display and selection of the various options.

Joysticks for directed scanning techniques or number pads for encoding techniques can also be used. In general, these types of interfaces involve not only significant hardware additions to the terminals, but also changes in the format and overall selection procedures. Although these techniques can be more efficient than some of the scanning techniques, they generally are not practical in terms of implementation in public access terminals. Individuals who regularly need and use these types of input techniques often have custom aids which they can use, and which could be interfaced to the terminals through an auxiliary keyboard port, as described above.

SUMMARY

A wide variety of techniques and procedures have been developed for providing rapid and effective means for input and control to individuals with different types of handicaps. For these approaches to be used in public access data entry terminals, however, a large number of considerations need to be made beyond those which pertain to the design of special aids for use strictly by handicapped individuals. Among these are cost, complexity, maintenance, additional training and setup time. Even with these constraints, however, there are simple, low-cost modifications which can be made to computer terminals to enhance their use by individuals having a wide variety of disabilities. Incorporation of these modifications can be done most easily at the initial design stages of the hardware and software for the system. Many of the techniques, however, can also be retrofitted at relatively low cost. When considering such modifications, either in the initial design or in retrofitting, it is important to contact professionals who have expertise in making similar modifications.

With careful thought and planning, low-cost and effective modifications can be made to the terminal to allow access by a large number of individuals who would otherwise be unable to use these systems. This can result not only in better access to these "public" terminals, but can also open up new job opportunities for handicapped individuals in developing and maintaining such databases or information systems.

ALLAN H. LEVY, M.D.
Professor of Computer Science and Clinical Sciences
University of Illinois at Urbana-Champaign

Resistance to Technology: Some Examples from the Health Care Delivery System

Understanding why people don't like something is like understanding why the dog *didn't* bark in the night. One is often looking for objections unspoken, fears unexpressed and concerns concealed. It is the purpose of this paper to attempt to explore some of the factors that are at work when radical changes are introduced into a new setting.* I will try to separate problems that arise from changes we introduce from those that derive from external factors. Finally, I will consider some of the ways by which we cannot only overcome the resistance that we meet in users, but take advantage of it by extracting from it important information on improving the system.

As examples, I will consider the introduction of technology into two different medical domains to user groups who have a reputation for some substantial degree of resistance to change: in the first case, clinical pathologists and laboratory technologists; in the second, physicians, nurses and others in a ward setting. I will discuss the differences encountered between the introduction of laboratory information systems and the introduction onto the ward of hospital information systems. These will illustrate some of the problems involved in promoting public use of information technology.

We have worked for many years with physicians trying to design hospital information systems that would be used not only for simple billing and bookkeeping, but used by physicians and other health professionals as a tool for patient care. This has led us to encourage hands-on

*Supported in part by a training grant from the National Library of Medicine, U.S. Public Health Service (NLM 07011).

117

participation of the health professional in the actual operation of the information system. We have tried to make our primary users—doctors, nurses, pharmacists—comfortable with automation. We have had limited success. An analysis of the limits reached and the problems encountered will be useful. Before beginning this analysis, however, I will set forth one simple but powerful postulate: it is more useful to find out why a tool does not work than simply to try to force its use.

In many cases, new developments—which seem so attractive to their developers—have flaws which are evident to nearly everyone else.[1] When these flaws are finally identified by the developer, it is a source of immense surprise that the problem was concealed for so long. In many cases, it was really a case of not wanting to think about the problems. It is not an easy task to evaluate your own work. It is often painful for the innovator to step back and ask, "What am I doing wrong?" This is not a question with which one is usually comfortable. However, it is generally pointless to try to persuade users to employ a new tool without understanding why they don't want to use it. It is only by perceptive analysis of those features of a system that disturb users that we can gain some insights into how to modify the system so it may be more useful.

I am asserting that assessment is a critical and integral part of the process of introducing new technology into public use. We frequently associate technology assessment with economic analysis, changes in cost that will accompany the substitution of one way of doing a task with another. If considered only in these terms, those involved with a development that is expected to bring new qualities to society—in particular, greater public access to knowledge—tend to take a dim view of such constrained economic assessment. However, a strict economic analysis is only a limited component of what comprehensive technology assessment should be. It should lead to a system-oriented viewpoint which will evaluate new developments not only from the vantage point of the developer, nor even that of the primary user alone, but also from those of others in society. As developers, we should not reject assessment, but rather try to use it to improve our products. Although some of the factors causing innovations to fail may be beyond the control of the developer, many others are amenable to changes and improvements, once the problem is identified.

Medical Information Systems—Their Promises and Their Problems

In the early 1960s, in the early days of information technology, there was very substantial enthusiasm for the use of computers and information systems in hospitals and in other components of the health care system. In order to put the picture in some perspective, it is useful to look at the scene as it was at that time, and also to note the changes then occurring within the health care system itself.

In the sixties the problems associated with health services were only beginning to emerge as a pressing national issue. Several factors predominated: there had been an enormous expansion in the capacity to provide effective and life-benefiting therapy with the advent of antibiotics, blood transfusions and new vaccinations. This was accompanied by rapid social changes emerging after World War II. There was a growing perception that medical services were not just a privilege open to the affluent few, but rather a national resource to be widely available to all social classes. The immediate result of this was a tremendous increase in demand for health care services. Just as we face today a biomedical information explosion, the sixties were a time of explosion in the actual delivery of medical and other health care services. Hospitals and other health delivery institutions were extremely ill-prepared for those drastic changes in the usual pattern of service delivery.[2]

The rise in basic medical research had not been accompanied by a study of ways to make such research benefits available to the people in the form of effective care. As a result, hospitals, starting from marginal efficiency, quickly found themselves in serious difficulties keeping up with the demand for expanded services.

The consequences were profound. Costs began to skyrocket as hospitals hired more and more personnel. Always a labor-intensive industry, health care was especially susceptible to damages through rapid expansion of its relatively inefficient, but very numerous, service personnel.

At this time, a variety of expensive diagnostic and analytic instruments were introduced. These added both to the costs and to the gross amount of information generated and the complexity of patient care. Foremost among these was the automatic laboratory analyzer. This single device has had as profound an influence on medical care, practice and costs as any other single development in the last two decades. Prior to the automatic clinical laboratory analyzer, laboratory tests were extraordinarily expensive. More than that, they were unreliable: the analytic instruments had such substantial variations that physicians were actually trained to ignore results of laboratory tests when they did not fit in with diagnostic impressions based on bedside observations. The high speed, accuracy and relatively low cost of tests performed with automatic analyzers changed that. The role of laboratory tests in clinical practice moved from a mistrusted ancillary to the very heart of the diagnostic process. Medical education changed rapidly to accommodate this new technology. The use and interpretation of laboratory tests became an important part of medical school and residency training. Physicians began to order tests not only to confirm suspicions, but to rule out previously unconsidered or unlikely possibilities. Mass screening became possible, and was instituted widely throughout the country.

Thus was technology of a high degree of sophistication introduced with considerable speed and with wide penetration. What was its impact? What was the extent and quality of the resistance to the introduction of automatic, high-speed laboratory analyzers? The resistance was, surprisingly enough, very scant in both duration and intensity. Pathologists could scarcely increase the capacity of their laboratories fast enough to run tests at a speed sufficient to satisfy the demand of the clinicians who ordered these tests. A widespread reliance on results, in terms of both diagnosis and future treatments, grew rapidly. Automatic analyzers of higher capacity and greater speed were developed. What resistance there was took the form of counsels of caution by medical educators. Such advice was heeded in the abstract, but largely ignored in practice. Senior internists continued for a time to warn against the "indiscriminate ordering of laboratory tests." However, the ever-increasing volume of tests actually ordered is evidence of the ineffectiveness of this attempt at maintaining parsimony and strict rationality in the ordering of laboratory tests.

It is worthwhile to examine some of the apparent reasons for the high degree of acceptance of laboratory automation. Possibly the most obvious single factor is the economic impact that automated testing has imposed. It has produced a high volume of increased activity—with accompanying revenue—for the clinical pathologist. It has not taken revenue away from another section of the medical profession. It initially added to the costs of care paid for by the patient or the patient's third-party payer.

It is often the case in medicine that technical developments in one area do not reduce the volume of activity in another; it is more likely that the new innovation will simply be a new service not previously supplied, ideally and presumably improving the quality of care.

Economic factors are probably among the most important relating to the acceptability of new developments. Where an innovation is in the economic self-interest of a group, it is likely to meet widespread acceptance within that group. Where that group controls its use, it is likely to gain widespread currency throughout society, unless opposing pressures are extremely strong. Several consequences follow from this economic determinism:

1. Resistance can be better understood in the light of an understanding of whose economic interests will be served and whose will be hurt.
2. Often the impact of a technological development is only considered and controlled by the group which will be benefited; others who may be adversely affected are frequently unaware of the impact of new developments on them until widespread changes are already in place.

When evaluating the public's access to automated stores of knowledge, we need to consider in detail who stands to benefit—but equally we should consider who stands to lose. We must weigh the benefits against the losses, and devise systems that will accommodate the desired social change with the least economic dislocations.

To return to the evolution of laboratory automation, what was the effect on the technologists? In general, laboratory automation was willingly accepted by most of the technicians in the field. The increased volume of operations brought far more prominence and visibility to their field. Their work became easier. The test results, which are their principal product, became trusted. Accordingly, their work achieved higher prestige, with higher job satisfaction. Laboratory technicians became elevated in both professional status and compensation.

What about loss of jobs due to automation? In this instance, this did not occur. Laboratory technology opened up a whole new industry. The job market for laboratory workers increased enormously. Here, then, is an example where technology was introduced, quickly accepted, and has had a tremendous impact on the substance of the health care system.

A principal conclusion is that where technology provides benefits without any immediate or apparent disadvantages, the fact that it is new is not an impediment to its acceptance, even in a conservative profession. A secondary lesson is this: the unhesitating acceptance of a new technological development may lead to its uncritical overutilization. As discussed earlier, there is a considerable concern in medical circles that laboratory tests are now substantially overused. There has been a sharp increase in malpractice claims. The rise of scientific medicine has led to a higher expectation of accuracy in diagnosis, and what is now termed "defensive medicine" is the common mode of medical operation. Since laboratory tests were introduced into common medical practice without any critical examination of the value or cost-effectiveness of any particular test or battery of tests (in essence, a shotgun approach was adopted), there is now no good measuring stick by which to gauge the value of the ever-growing use of the laboratory. Overuse of the clinical lab is a significant factor in the cycle of rising medical costs.

The Introduction of Technology to the Ward—A Model of Cyclic Resistance

Earlier it was mentioned that the rise in demand for health services had placed sudden and severe strains on the ability of hospitals to provide needed in-patient services. This was partially due to a shortage of physicians, and in the sixties this was dealt with by direct means—namely, increasing both the number of medical students per school and the number of medical schools in the United States. The effect of this change was not to be felt for a number of years. Consequently, hospitals were called upon to take more rapid action to handle the immediate burden. Research programs designed to improve the delivery of health care were started. Information flow in hospitals and inefficiencies in medical record systems were recognized early as serious problems. Not only did lost or missing medical records interfere with the treatment of an individual patient, but a missing medical record would trigger a spreading train of confusion and wasted effort. A temporary record would have to be set up, and messengers would be dispatched to various sites where the record might have been mislocated. Tests would have to be repeated if the earlier results were lost.

It is hard to document the amount of the economic loss attributable to lost medical records in the wards and clinics of large hospitals. However, in the early sixties, it was estimated that in one large Eastern university-operated hospital, one out of four requests for a medical record was answered with a "cannot locate" response. In addition, hospitals had no ready administrative control over their pharmacy costs and other ancillary patient care services. Manual methods of ordering drugs and services were not adequately linked with the billing systems. Substantial numbers of charges were lost, or so delayed in posting to patient accounts that bill collection and cash flow were seriously impaired.

In the face of all this, it is no surprise that the hospital was a prime target for the introduction of computer-based information systems. It is hard to imagine now the enthusiasm that preceded and accompanied the earliest stages of hospital "computerization." Hospital administrators were sufficiently concerned about, and crippled by, their information management problems that they saw in the computer a magic answer to their problems. This enthusiasm was very short-lived. It soon became apparent that the development of hospital information systems presented problems in several domains, none of which had been adequately anticipated:

1. The hardware needed for a real-time, on-line system was not yet sufficiently reliable.
2. The software that would permit the rapid development of new programs, and their easy modification in response to user criticisms, was not available. Assembler languages were still the standard for production programming, and high-level languages which easily accommodated text manipulation were not in common use.
3. Hospital functions were not understood in detail sufficient to permit precise specification of a hospital information system.
4. The management of large information system projects had not yet been adequately explored. The importance of user consultation in advance of

design specification may have been known, but was not commonly practiced. All too often, systems were set forth by the programmer-analyst, cast in concrete by the coder, then sent forth for the first time for the inspection of the user.

With these deficiencies, it is no surprise that early hospital information systems almost universally ran into serious opposition from their various user constituencies. Nurses were called upon in many cases to be the direct users of the systems. Ill-trained in administration, but with increasing management tasks thrust upon them, head nurses now had either to enter data directly or to supervise the clerks who did. With the system deficiencies outlined above, this additional task was time-consuming and frustrating. Since no discernible benefits accrued to the nursing service from the information system, there was no accompanying motivation to use the system.

The physicians and other professionals involved similarly viewed early systems as impediments—as part of the problem, rather than as steps to the solution. Of course, there were exceptions; some medical professionals became enthusiastic about the potential benefits of the system—the opportunity to have clinical information available for research, the chance to have an adequate data base for planning rational treatment, the potential for more effective uses of hospital personnel resources. These intended benefits were the raison d'être for hospital information systems, unrealized as they were.

The result of these unmatched expectations was predictable. Medical information systems lost their charm to physicians and hospital administrators alike. Interest in developing them dropped sharply, both on the part of medical researchers and commercial software companies, as it became apparent that success in such efforts was unlikely. Progress in the field slowed considerably, with the exception of continued efforts in computer-based hospital billing. Medical information was viewed by the developers of such systems as primarily data that reflected fiscal events, rather than from the point of view of their medical content.

Thus, another wave of growth followed, this one emphasizing the accounting, business and collection (ABCs) aspects of hospital operations. This, in general, is the present state today. Several large vendors sell business-oriented hospital information systems. These are largely successful in helping hospitals capture charges. In the process, they also facilitate more complete and timely processing of orders to laboratories and pharmacies. Thus, they do benefit medical care indirectly. But they are largely insufficient in terms of their potential medical content, and they have not reached the goal of aiding more rational medical treatment as was originally set forth.

Within the past year, however, the availability of inexpensive micro-processers, and the ability of hospital clinics to devise special-purpose information systems tailored to their individual medical needs, has instituted still another wave of developments. Small, medically oriented information modules are becoming increasingly prevalent in hospital and clinic environments. These are meeting with much less user resistance than did the earlier systems. A major reason for their acceptance is that they work. Although this sounds like a truism, it is probably the most powerful factor compelling acceptance of an innovation. If it produces the promised results—even at a higher cost—it will usually be accepted. Also, the new systems are often either locally designed or skillfully tailored to local needs. This direct personal involvement is a powerful force stimulating acceptance. (But it should be realized that the personal involvement of the user in the creation of a system can lead to noncritical acceptance of a system that really is not demonstrably effective.) Finally, the reduced cost and intrinsic higher reliability of new computers has been a significant factor in promoting the success of recent developments.

Thus, after a poor start, with resulting emphasis on predominantly fiscal functions, changes in technology have again brought forth a new wave of developments.[3] Now, medical information systems are being recreated with increasing success and with new emphasis on clinical decision support. Resistance can be overcome by the personal involvement of the users and by improvement in the intrinsic quality of the tools of technology.

Summary

The attitude of society to technology is still difficult to predict. This is disappointing to innovators, if not surprising to analysts. Society—or even smaller segments of it, such as the health services community—has no single common goal and no agreement on the weighting of utility values. Thus, the first step in introducing any new technological development is to decide in advance what the expected goals are and to set forth the expected benefits and anticipated losses. No technological innovation is an unequivocal blessing. There may not be universal agreement with stated goals, but at least their explicit existence provides a bench mark against which to judge the success or failure of an innovation.

Although an analysis of economic benefits for the involved groups will be a powerful predictor of the attitude of those groups to a technical innovation, other, less tangible factors are involved as well. The perception by an individual of the status of his job is an important determinant in the success of a system. The participation of users in the design of a system will help ensure their cooperation in its implementation. However, such involvement may lead to uncritical acceptance, and may bias cost-effectiveness analysis. In spite of this, user involvement is the single most powerful technique that can be used to ensure system success.

REFERENCES

1. Nolan, Richard L. "Restructuring the Data Processing Organization for Data Resource Management." *In* Bruce Gilchrist, ed. *Information Processing 77* (IFIP Congress Series, vol. 7). New York, North-Holland, 1977, pp. 261-65.

2. Collen, Morris F., ed. *Hospital Computer Systems*. New York, Wiley, 1974.

3. U.S. Congress. Office of Technology Assessment. *Policy Implications of Medical Information Systems*. Washington, D.C., USGPO, 1977.

INDEX

Adaptation, to computer systems, 45.
Algorithmic method of design, 4.
Alternate keyboards. *See* Keyboards, alternate.
Auditory displays, for computer terminals, 101.
Automatic laboratory analyzer, 119-20.
Automation, in hospitals, 121-22.
Auto-monitoring technique, 102, 115.

Baseline study, for IIDA, 63-65.
BROWSE system, 77-98; example of search, 80-89.
Browsing, in machine-readable databases, 77-98.

C-DEK terminals, 38.
Canned searches, for instructional purposes, 52.
Catalog equipment, 20-36.
Category perspicuity, 92.
Circulation policies, 43.
Cognitive processing difficulties, for handicapped, 109.
COM catalog, 45-46.
Command-driven system, 47.
Computer-assisted instruction, 51-54.
Computer-naïve users, 77-98.
Computer naïveté, types of, 78.
Computer terminals: design of, for handicapped, 99-100; determination of number needed, 20-36, 46-47; interactive, 8-19; public, 44; types of, for handicapped, 99-116. *See also* C-DEK terminals; Remote access terminals; Talking terminals.
Computing Review classification, 81-82.

Dallas Public Library, study of traffic at catalog, 21-36.
Database, frame. *See* Frame database.
Database, record. *See* Record database.
Deaf persons, and use of computer terminals, 99.
Defensive medicine, 121.
Design: and values, 4-7; constraints on, for computer terminals for handicapped, 110-11; fallacies of, 12-19;

major elements of, 8-11; of computer terminals for handicapped, 99-100; of on-line circulation systems, 41-43; of public access information systems, 2-7, 78; principles of, for search diagnosis, 56-57.
Design, algorithmic method of. *See* Algorithmic method of design.
Design, heuristic method of. *See* Heuristic method of design.
Design, simulation method of. *See* Simulation method of design.
Diagnosis: of searching techniques, 55-57; of user performance, future research directions, 74-75.
Diagnostic procedures, for IIDA, 58-62.
Diagnostic tests, performance of, for user performance, 71-74.
DIALOG, 50-76.
Direct selection, technique for physically handicapped, 101-02, 113.
DOBIS system (file structuring), 41.
Dwelling (search behavior), 61-62.

Encoding techniques, for increasing selection space, 107-09.
Exxon Research and Engineering Company: at Florham Park, N.J., 63-65; at Linden, N.J., 65-68.
Eye position sensing system, for handicapped persons, 102.

Feedback, as element of heuristic approach to design, 5.
File design, for on-line circulation system, 41.
Files, wrapped, 43.
Fill description, 95.
Frame database, 94-96.
Frames, in BROWSE, 80-81.

Gandalf network (University of Guelph), 44-45.
GEAC, 41; GEAC 800, 44; GEAC 8000, 42-45.
Group description, 95.
Guelph, University of. *See* University of Guelph.

126